Lighting
for Interior Design

Published in 2012
by Laurence King Publishing Ltd
361–373 City Road
London EC1V 1LR
Tel +44 20 7841 6900
E enquiries@laurenceking.com
www.laurenceking.com

ISBN 978 1 85669 836 8
Designed by John Round Design
Printed in the UK

Laurence King Publishing is committed to ethical and sustainable
production. We are proud participants in The Book Chain Project
bookchainproject.com

Title page: One Gyle Square, Edinburgh, lighting design by FOTO-MA
Opposite: Section drawing of lighting scheme for the Musée de
l'Orangerie, Paris, by Anne Bureau Concepteur Lumière

Lighting
for Interior Design

Malcolm Innes

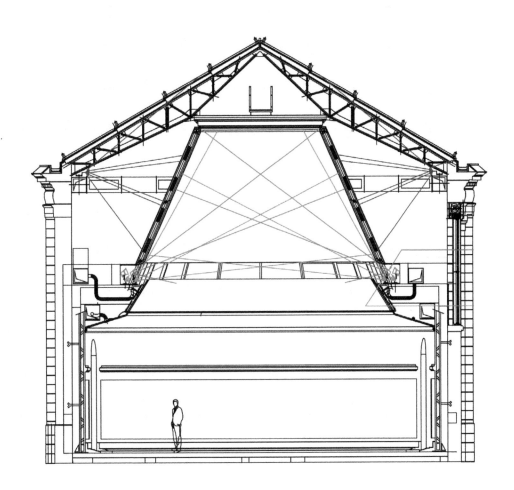

Laurence King Publishing

Contents

Related study material is available on the Laurence King website at
www.laurenceking.com

Introduction

'A common man marvels at uncommon things; a wise man marvels at the commonplace.'
CONFUCIUS

Light surrounds us every day; it is the epitome of 'commonplace', and this familiarity can prevent us seeing its wonder. It affects our sleep patterns and working hours, our alertness and health. Yet the power and importance of light are often overlooked by those who shape our built environment. Hopefully, this book will encourage readers to marvel at the commonplace and so help them produce great architecture.

The word 'vision' has grown beyond its Latin roots (from the word *videre* meaning 'to see'). 'Vision' now includes all that can be imagined and dreamt. But it still also defines the act of seeing – and it is light that makes the world visible, and light that allows us to make sense of our surroundings. Despite this, the importance of light in architecture is often underestimated. Great architecture and interior design thrill the senses, but consider how little of our built environment is experienced in any way other than through our sense of sight. Without light, interior architecture simply cannot be fully experienced; it is invisible to us. However, light can influence much more than just our visual experience of architecture.

Light reveals colour and three-dimensional form, while directional plays of light expose the texture of surfaces and materials. These elements are so integral to the appreciation of space that without the carefully considered and appropriate application of light, interior design can never be truly great.

Light has the power to influence the mood and atmosphere of space. Altering the patterns of light, shade and colour can make the users feel relaxed or alert; warm and comfortable; cold and uneasy. Light and colour can be used to make users feel stimulated or subdued. Skilful use of light allows us to imbue interior designs with the sensations and emotions we want users to experience.

Given the importance of light and colour within interior design, it is surprising how often lighting seems accidental and extraneous. Light is intangible and immaterial, which seems to imply that it is also uncontrollable, but interior design is fundamentally about the manipulation of space – another immaterial property.

As with architecture and interior design, lighting design is neither an art nor a science, but a synthesis of both. It is a subject that is often clouded by technical terms, complex physics and mathematics. But at its core lies a simple truth: we were all born with an innate appreciation of light and colour, and all our favourite built environments draw deeply from that well of experience.

Left
Musée de l'Orangerie, Paris. Lighting by Anne Bureau Concepteur Lumière. Careful lighting design was integral to the success of this gallery conversion.

About this book

This book is an introduction to the subject of architectural lighting design. It intends to explore the aesthetic and emotional capabilities of well-designed lighting without obscuring the subject behind science and mathematical formulas. Dramatic and visually stunning projects are illustrated throughout, but this is not just a picture book. The work of some of the world's leading lighting design practices is analyzed in detail to explore some fundamental principles of this field.

The book is divided into two parts. The first part, Theory, explains the physical properties of light and its physical and psychological effects on humans. It outlines elements of natural and artificial light, including a discussion of types of luminaire and control systems. The second part, Process and Practice, first covers practical lighting principles, good design for human needs, and how to light surfaces and spaces. It then focuses on the practicalities of presentation for clients and others: how to record lighting systems, and communication from initial sketches and test models through to providing specifications for contractors and the all-important on-site finalization. All these elements are crucial in realizing a successful lighting design project.

Above, right
Copenhagen Opera House interior, lighting by Speirs and Major Associates. Good lighting design not only enhances occupants' experience of an interior space, but can also, as in this case, help visitors move through a space.

Right
Copenhagen Opera House. A good designer will also consider how lighting affects a building's exterior.

PART I THEORY

1. The physics of light

Light elicits both physical and emotional reactions from human beings. We have a 'human' response to light. But in objective and scientific terms, what is light? Even in the objective world of the scientist, light is often confusing and contradictory. The nature of light has been a subject of philosophical and scientific enquiry for centuries. Man has been trying to identify it since the time before mathematics and physics.

Despite thousands of years of human enquiry, remarkably little was understood about light beyond its basic observable features before the eighteenth century. It was observed that light travels in a straight line; that polished surfaces such as mirrors reflect light; and that crossing beams of light do not interfere with each other. It was not until Sir Isaac Newton published *Opticks: A Treatise on the Reflections, Refractions, Inflections and Colours of Light* in 1704 that the true nature of white light was widely understood.

However, the greatest leap in the understanding of light was achieved in the nineteenth century by the physicist James Clerk Maxwell. His 1864 work entitled *A Dynamic Theory of the Electro-Magnetic Field* established the fundamental truth of light: that light is energy.

As Albert Einstein observed, 'The work of James Clerk Maxwell changed the world forever.' Einstein had no doubts about the importance of Clerk Maxwell's work to his own; he described the physicist's work as, 'the most profound and the most fruitful that physics has experienced since the time of Newton'.[1] For a medium that governs so much of our lives, two remarkably simple questions can demonstrate how little most of us know about the nature of light: 'What is light?' and 'What is colour?'

1 'James Clerk Maxwell' in *Encyclopædia Britannica*, 2010, Encyclopædia Britannica Online, 4 May, 2010, http://www.britannica.com/EBchecked/topic/370621/James-Clerk-Maxwell

Right
Industrial lasers can concentrate vast amounts of light into a very small area, creating enough energy to cut through sheet steel.

What is light?

Light, as we have said, is energy. It is part of the electromagnetic spectrum that includes radio waves, microwaves, X-rays, infrared and ultraviolet. These are all forms of electromagnetic radiation, the difference being in the wavelength (and therefore energy level) of the radiation. Visible light is simply that: visible energy. It is electromagnetic energy in a range that our visual system is sensitive to and that gives us the sensation of sight. In contrast, although infrared radiation is also electromagnetic radiation, our eyes are not sensitive to it. We get no sensation of sight from infrared; instead, we perceive it as heat.

As light is a form of energy it obeys physical laws that apply to energy, including the laws of thermodynamics. The first law of thermodynamics states that energy cannot be created or destroyed; it can only be transformed from one kind of energy into another. Light can be produced with heat, where an object becomes so hot that it radiates energy as light. Light can be produced by the transformation of chemical energy. Visible light can also be produced by the transformation of other kinds of electromagnetic energy, such as ultraviolet or microwave energy.

There is evidence all around us of the energy embodied in light. Solar cells transform the energy in visible light to electrical energy; industrial laser cutters are used to cut intricate patterns in everything from delicate paper to the toughest steel plates. But the most ubiquitous transformation of light energy is found among plants. Plants use the power of visible light to convert carbon dioxide and water into food (a process called photosynthesis). The human visual system converts light energy entering the eyes into chemical energy that is used to communicate the information received by the eye to the brain.

Below
Visible light is just a small part of the spectrum of electromagnetic radiation, which includes X-rays, microwaves and radio waves. Radiation with wavelengths between about 380 and 750 nm is the only part of the spectrum that we perceive as light. Infrared energy is experienced as heat.

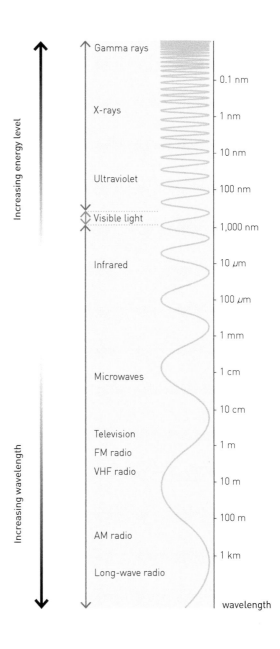

The physical properties of light – what designers need to know

Although this book is about designing with light, and is not a physics textbook, we need to understand some basic properties of light before we can use it effectively in the built environment. The more we understand about the physical properties of light, the easier it becomes to use it creatively.

The most basic property of light is that it travels in straight lines if it does not encounter other materials. Also, a beam of light is invisible to us unless it strikes materials such as a solid surface or dust; it becomes visible when it hits something that reflects some light towards our eyes. Materials that we would describe as white or light-coloured appear so because they reflect more light than dark ones. (However, it is not simply the quantity of light we put into a space that makes it seem bright. It is the reflective properties of the surfaces in that space. A black-painted room will always appear dark, no matter how much light we put into it.)

Polished surfaces produce specular reflections. Specular means 'like a mirror', and a good specular reflection will not distort the beam of light. This enables us to have mirrors that give us an image of ourselves as others see us. Specular reflectors maintain the integrity of a beam of light, and light striking the reflector at an angle will be reflected at an equal and opposite angle. If we shine a torch at a mirror, we have to look at the mirror from the correct angle to see the reflection of the torch beam.

Very matt surfaces produce diffuse reflections. A perfectly diffuse reflector will reflect light equally from all angles. A sheet of plain white printing paper is close to being a perfectly diffuse reflector. The light beam is disrupted when it hits the surface of a diffuse reflector and light hitting the surface at an angle loses any direction in the reflection. Whatever direction we see the sheet from, it appears to be equally bright.

A common misconception is that shiny surfaces reflect more light than matt ones. This is not necessarily true; the difference lies in the direction in which the surface reflects the light. The mirror could appear dark when viewed from a position where the light source cannot be seen, while if the white paper is lit by a torch it appears equally bright wherever we view it from.

Light travels in a straight line, but when it moves from one transparent medium to another its path can be bent. This process is called refraction and happens when light passes between materials of different optical density (measured as the refractive index). A shaped glass lens will bend light travelling from the air through the glass to bring it to a focus at some point beyond the lens.

TIP OPAQUE MATERIALS

Despite frequent misuse, the term 'opaque' only has one meaning; opaque materials are not transparent and cannot be seen through – they pass no light. When most people say 'opaque' they actually mean 'translucent'. A translucent material, such as etched glass or tracing paper, does not permit clear vision, but does allow some light through – it is semi-transparent. Therefore, it is essential when speaking about light to use this terminology correctly and to question others closely to determine what they actually mean. After all, a truly opaque window is rather pointless, but frosted or etched glass has many uses.

REFLECTION

It is the interaction between light and surfaces that defines our visual impression of materials, objects and spaces. Without light, surfaces remain unseen, and without a surface to interrupt a beam of light, the light itself remains unseen. A simple change of wall covering or the addition of a mirror or glazed painting can dramatically alter the lit appearance of a space. An understanding and consideration of reflection is therefore an essential component of any lighting design.

1 A standard glass mirror is a good approximation for a perfect reflector. Following the laws of reflection, a beam of light hitting the mirror at an angle will be reflected back at the equal and opposite angle. This is a specular reflection.

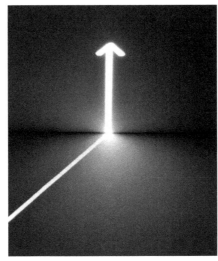

2 White paper only produces a soft reflection. Although the light hits the surface at an angle, the reflection has no direction. The light is reflected pretty equally in all directions. This is a diffuse reflection.

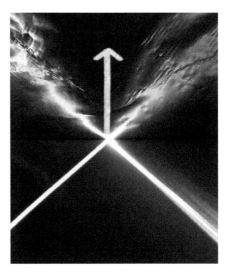

3 Polished aluminium can produce specular reflections like a mirror. If the polish is not perfect or the surface is not absolutely flat, the reflected image will be imperfect.

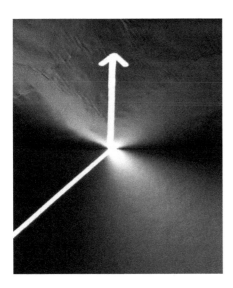

4 A non-polished reflective surface, such as (unpolished) mill finish aluminium, is halfway between a perfect reflector and a diffuser. The resulting soft, diffuse reflection can still have a real direction to the beam. This is described as a semi-specular reflector.

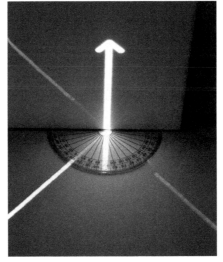

5 A glazed ceramic tile produces a diffused reflection from its white pigment and a specular reflection from the glaze. In this image, the light hitting the ceramic tile has produced a soft glow over the ground plane as well as a distinct reflected line on the right of the picture. The bright angled line on the left of the tile is a reflection of the incoming beam of light on the ground.

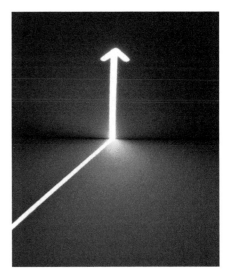

6 Whether it is polished or matt, a coloured surface will impart some of its colour to the reflected light. The beam of light that hits the orange wall is white, but the reflected light on the floor is tinted with the colour of the wall.

MIRRORS

Although lenses are used in many types of lighting equipment, the majority of luminaires use reflectors to control the direction and spread of light from a source. Most reflectors are made from polished aluminium or mirror-coated plastic. Flat, perfectly mirrored surfaces are rarely used as they require great accuracy in the positioning of a light source. Instead, combinations of curved mirrors and textured surfaces are used to produce a more even spread of light. Non-perfect reflectors are favoured as they allow greater tolerance in the positioning of a light source and so produce less variation between different luminaires.

1 This curved Mylar sheet has a mirror-like finish. The curve means the incoming, parallel beams of light hit the reflective surface at different angles and this produces the pattern of reflection. Here the parallel beams of light are entering from the lower left of the picture and are being reflected to meet at a point in front of the curved reflector – the focus of the curve. It is easy to see that, with a light source placed at the focus point, a parallel beam of light would be produced by this reflector shape.

2 Lighting reflectors are often made from materials that are not perfectly flat mirrors. This aluminium sample has a mirrored finish, but it is also highly textured. This produces a specular reflection but the patterning introduces some variation to this, which widens the spread of light and also introduces some sparkle where light is reflected towards the viewer. Textured materials such as this are often used in luminaire reflectors to 'soften' light from very intense sources.

TRANSPARENCY

Light can pass through various materials, and these are described as being transparent. With most such materials, we tend to think that all light passes through, and indeed a physical definition of transparency is that heat or electromagnetic radiation can pass through without distortion. However, even window glass interferes with light, only transmitting a proportion of the light striking it and completely blocking parts of the non-visible spectrum. Nevertheless, transparent materials are an essential feature of our built environment; to design with light you must understand how it interacts with these materials.

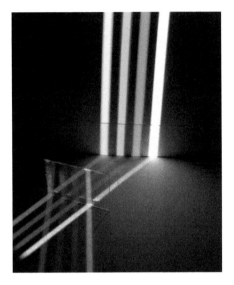

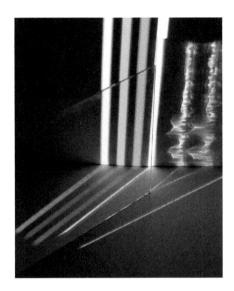

1 A transparent material can never pass 100% of the light that hits it. The polished surface of this piece of thin acrylic sheet reflects some of this light. Normal window glass typically transmits a maximum of around 80% of the visible light that reaches it.

2 The more acute the angle of the incoming light, the more light will be reflected. In this example, a sheet of glass is set at a very acute angle to the beam of white light. Most of this light is reflected by the glass, resulting in a significantly darker line of transmitted light.

3 At some point, the incident angle of the light becomes so shallow that no light can pass straight through the transparent material and all the light is reflected. Where the light is directed at a very shallow angle into the edge of a transparent material such as this sheet of glass, the light is reflected by the inside surfaces and bounces along the length of the sheet to emerge at the other end. In this case, the light is distorted by imperfections in the surface of the glass. It has also taken on a green tint after travelling through the equivalent of a 150 mm-thick piece of glass.

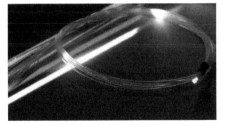

4 This acrylic rod interrupts the green beam of light and, through internal reflection, the light is transported along the rod to emerge at the other end.

5 Fibre-optic cables are designed to redirect light by the process of total internal reflection. Rather than using one large rod, fibre-optic cables are usually made from a number of smaller strands. This gives them great flexibility and allows them to be bent into tight curves without losing light. This small bunch of plastic fibre optics captures some of the light from the green, blue and red beams of light and transports it along the whole length of the strand to emerge at the other end. Fibre optics for lighting are very good at transmitting visible light, but poor at transmitting infrared (heat). This feature allows a hot light source to be separated from heat-sensitive materials that are to be illuminated.

FILTERS AND LENSES

Many materials transmit more light than they reflect. We tend to call most such materials 'transparent', but transparent materials still filter transmitted light to some degree. Window glass tints light with a very subtle green tinge. The thicker the glass, the more it will tint the light. Other materials impart strong colours, diffuse light or otherwise alter beams of light in some way. Designers can harness these material properties to control the colour and spread of light within their designs.

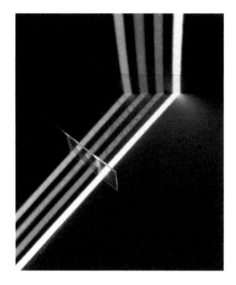

1 Clear transparent materials allow light to pass through without significantly altering the colour or spread of the light.

2 The term 'opaque' is often misused, but it has only one meaning. Opaque materials prevent any light passing through. This image shows an opaque card interrupting the beams of light and casting a shadow onto the wall beyond.

3 Translucent materials like frosted glass, tracing paper or the theatrical filter used in this image allow light to pass through but diffuse the beam. Different materials diffuse the beam to different extents; this theatrical diffusion filter produces beams that are very indistinct at any significant distance beyond the filter.

4 This theatrical filter is a light frost and, like a lightly etched piece of glass, it softens the beams of light a little but the beams remain distinct. This level of diffusion is not suitable for creating a light box or backlit panel, as the lamps would be clearly visible.

5 Coloured transparent materials allow light of certain colours to pass through, while blocking other colours. This theatrical filter allows red light to pass through. The green, red and white beams all have some red light in them, so this passes through while the other colours are absorbed by the filter. The blue light contains no red, so no light passes through the filter.

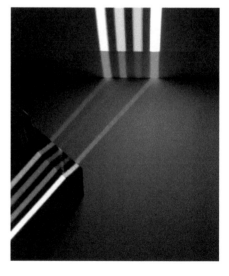

6 This green-coloured filter absorbs all the colours apart from green. The red light here contains very little green light and therefore appears very dim compared to the other colours.

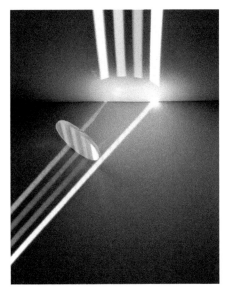

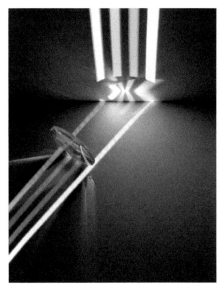

7 While the green, blue and white light beams all contain some blue light, the red beam has no blue light and is greatly darkened by the blue-coloured filter. A very small amount of light is visible in the red beam, but this is largely because the filter material is not a perfect blue and is not a good block to the infrared part of the spectrum. This allows a little bit of visible red light through, which mixes with the general wash of blue to make a dim purple band where the red line should be.

8 This sample of frosted glass does not completely diffuse the light, but it produces a very soft-edged beam of light on the wall behind. This kind of diffusion filter is designed to soften the beam of a narrow spotlight.

9 This transparent convex lens bends the light to an equal extent in all directions, creating a circular beam of light.

11 This glass filter is transparent but is cut into a fluted shape on one side. Acting like a set of cylindrical lenses, this filter spreads the light in one plane creating an elliptical beam of light. This kind of lens is often used to spread the light of a circular spotlight to effectively illuminate tall objects in museum displays; hence it is commonly known as a sculpture lens or simply as a spread lens.

10 This cylindrical acrylic rod acts like a two-dimensional lens. Light is refracted by the lens, but only in one plane. The white beam of light has been spread horizontally but not vertically by the lens.

Right Diagram illustrating how the investigations illustrated on these pages were achieved using a digital projector.

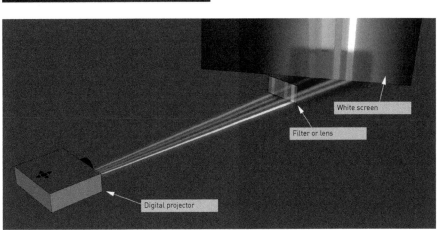

White screen

Filter or lens

Digital projector

REFRACTION

Light travels in a straight line, but when it passes obliquely through transparent materials of different densities, it can be deflected. The extent of the deflection is determined by the density of the elements through which the light passes (such as glass and air) and the angle at which the light meets the surface of the transparent material. This process of refraction allows our eyes to bend the light passing through our pupils so that it is focused on the retina at the rear of the eye. Refraction also allows us to create lenses that bend and deflect beams of light in such devices as DVD players, telescopes and projectors.

1 This glass of water refracts the focused beam of light, spreading it out into a blurred pattern on the surfaces beyond. The amount of refraction is affected by the angle at which the light hits the surface of the object. The varying curves on the glass bend the light to different extents.

2 At this angle, the acrylic prism produces both reflected and refracted images. Some of the light reflects off the polished surface and hits the rear wall on the left. Some of the light enters the prism and is refracted so that it comes out at a different angle and hits the rear wall on the right. Lenses work by refraction – bending the light to give the light beam a new direction.

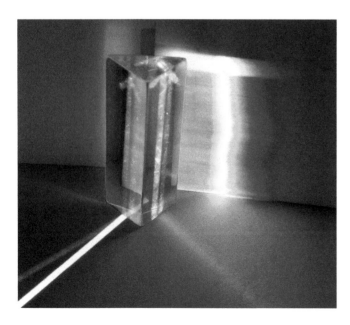

3 The refraction process actually bends the different wavelengths of light by different extents. In this image, the line of white light is smeared by the prism to show its component colours.

SHADOWS

It is often overlooked, but designing a lighting scheme also means designing the location and depth of shadows. Lighting design is not about eliminating shadows, rather making best use of them. A great deal of information about the light in a space can be inferred by the nature of a shadow: the number of light sources, their locations, the direction in which they focus their light, their relative intensities and their distance from an object. Shadows are a vital clue that our visual system uses to interpret the three-dimensional shape and texture of objects in our field of view.

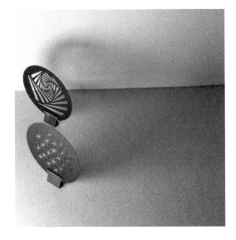

1 A diffuse light source close to these perforated patterns barely casts a shadow. The star pattern is about halfway between the light source and the wall beyond.

2 Move the light source a little further away and shadows begin to appear. The sharpness of a shadow is proportional to distance, so the relative distances between light source, pattern and the surface beyond affect the quality of the shadow. Notice that the pattern closest to the rear wall casts the clearest shadow – the distance from light source to pattern is much greater than from pattern to wall.

3 Move the light source even further back and the shadows become more distinct.

4 Even with a very diffused light source, a sharp shadow can be created if the distance between the source and the object is many times greater than the distance from the object to the surface beyond. In this case, the distance ratio for the star pattern is about 10:1.

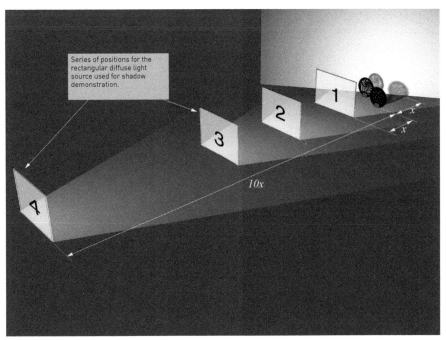

Series of positions for the rectangular diffuse light source used for shadow demonstration.

What is colour?

Colour is an incredibly important feature of our visual world, yet it is very difficult to describe what it is. Not only is colour difficult to define, it does not exist in the way we tend to think of it. At the most basic level, we respond to different wavelengths of light with the sensation of colour. Isaac Newton's famous experiments with sunlight and prisms – replicated in every rainbow – proved that white light is a mixture of colours.

We often think of colour as an intrinsic feature of an object or material – the rind of an orange is orange-coloured and a red car is red-coloured. But this is not the whole story: there are conditions when the orange and the car do not appear to be the colours we expect. When we say a car is red, what we actually mean is that under white light conditions the paint pigment on the car reflects mostly red light. This is an important variance on how we usually describe colour and objects.

Right
When white light is passed through a glass prism, the different wavelengths of visible light are spread out so that we can see the individual colours that were combined to make the white light.

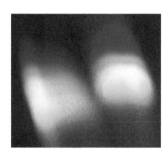

Above
A rainbow produces the same effect as a prism. Raindrops in the sky bend the different wavelengths of sunlight to different extents, which leads to the characteristic arcs of colour in the sky.

Right
The whole of the electromagnetic spectrum is made up of different wavelengths of radiation that have different properties. The small section of radiation we perceive as visible light covers a range of wavelengths from around 380 to 750 nm. Within that band, different wavelengths give the sensation of different colours, with red centred around 700 nm, green around 530 nm and blue around 470 nm.

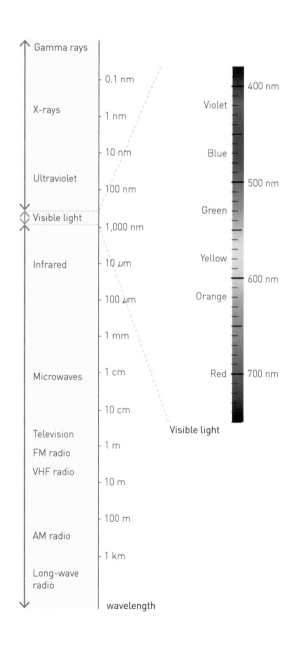

Gamma rays

X-rays — 0.1 nm

1 nm

10 nm

Ultraviolet — 100 nm

Visible light — 1,000 nm

Infrared — 10 μm

100 μm

1 mm

Microwaves — 1 cm

10 cm

Television

FM radio — 1 m

VHF radio

10 m

100 m

AM radio

1 km

Long-wave radio

wavelength

400 nm — Violet

Blue

500 nm — Green

Yellow

600 nm — Orange

Red — 700 nm

Visible light

Above

This children's toy is made of brightly coloured components. The various parts would normally be described as being red, white, blue, green or yellow.

A However, this description is based on what the toy looks like under white light.

B When lit with only red light, the colours of the components seem to shift, with the blue and green parts becoming much darker and the yellow taking on an orange hue.

C All the colours are still discernible under a pale green light, but they seem to have become anaemic and have lost all their vibrancy.

D Under strong blue light the components lose almost all sense of their white-light colours. The green roof and yellow bucket appear to be the same colour, and the blue body and white window look as though they could be the same material. The red tyres are totally unrecognizable.

Top
The apples only display their green and red colours under white light.

Centre
Using coloured light turns the green apple orange.

Bottom
Seen under a deep blue light, the red apple becomes very dark and looks more like a plum than an apple.

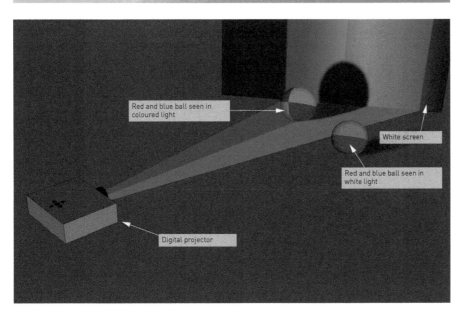

Left

The top image shows a coloured juggling ball illuminated with a single white light source, while in the bottom image the light source is filtered to be blue on the left and red on the right. As white light contains all the colours of visible light, the juggling ball can be seen as an object made from panels of different-coloured materials (top). The pigment in the top panel reflects red light most strongly and the front panel reflects blue light most strongly; under white light, we see these panels as red- and blue-coloured materials. However, when the same ball is seen under pale blue and pale red light (bottom), there is a remarkable transformation. When the top panel is illuminated by a blue light, which contains no red component, the material becomes dark. Under the red light, the top panel reflects red and so retains its colour. Under the red light, the front panel has no blue light to reflect and so it also becomes dark. In this example, the colours of the two lights are such that the top panel in blue light becomes a very close match for the front panel in red light – simply changing the lighting has completely altered our perception of these materials. We tend to believe that the colours we see in this toy are an inherent feature of the materials the toy is made from; in fact, the colours we see are a feature of the light that illuminates the object.

Quantifying light

We have a remarkable visual system that performs consistently over a wide range of lighting conditions, but there is one thing it cannot do: it cannot enable us to measure quantities of light just by looking.

We often talk about 'brightness' as if it is some form of measurement, but the best that can be said is that brightness is a perception, not an absolute. A single candle flame in a dark room appears to be very bright, but can hardly be seen in daylight. The sensation of brightness is also subjective. A person who has spent a lunch hour in a dimly lit restaurant may perceive some areas of the space as being quite bright. Meanwhile, another person walking in from the sunny street outside will see the whole restaurant as being dark.

What we think of as our inbuilt brightness scale is a contrast measurement, a relative assessment based on the surrounding light conditions and the conditions we have recently experienced. What is most remarkable about this is that our inbuilt assessment is constantly adjusting to suit our surroundings. This allows us to move between very light and very dark spaces, but prevents us having any real sense of measurable quantities of light.

Luckily, there are standardized measurements of light that do not rely on personal judgement. Unfortunately, they are standard physical units and the definitions can be quite complex. The descriptions presented here are simplified and are as technical as is necessary in this book. All lighting units are interlinked, so despite the simplifications some definitions can be difficult to decipher without reading other terms. Hopefully, a couple of readings will make things clear, and further information can easily be found in printed and online dictionaries.

Luminance

When we describe the 'brightness' of a lit surface, we are trying to describe the amount of light that emanates from it. Luminance is the accepted term for this and is an expression of the intensity of light emitted by a surface. It is related to the sensation of viewing a lit surface and, as such, the measurement relates to the angle of view of the eye looking at the surface. The SI unit (International System of Units) for luminance is candela per square metre (cd/^{2}).

Candela

The candela (cd) is an SI unit that quantifies luminous intensity in a given direction. Even before the advent of electric light there were attempts to standardize light sources, and these were measured against the light of a 'standard candle'. This early measurement system lingers on in the word 'candela', as one unit is roughly equivalent to the light of one standard candle. The candle flame radiates light in all directions; the candela also relates to the spherical radiance of light. 1 candela = 1 lumen per steradian (a conical angle within a sphere). A full sphere has a solid angle of 4 π steradians. For a light source, such as the standard candle, that produces 1 candela in all directions, this is equivalent to about 12.57 lumens.

Lumen

The lumen (lm) is an SI unit of luminous flux. It is a description of the quantity of light either produced by a source or received by a surface. One lumen is the quantity of luminous flux within a solid angle of this type of steradian emitted by a light source that has a luminous intensity of 1 candela.

Luminous flux

This is a measure of the total amount of light emitted by a light source or received by a lit surface. The SI unit for luminous flux is the lumen. Luminous flux is not a simple measurement of an amount of electromagnetic energy: it is weighted to match the sensitivity of the human visual system to different wavelengths of visible light.

Lux

Lux (lx) is the SI unit used to describe the illuminance of a surface – the amount of light that falls on it. It is not a measure of the luminance of a surface, i.e. how much light is emitted. Instead it is a measure of the illuminance of the surface. Lux quantifies the luminous flux within a surface area of 1 square metre. 1 lux = 1 lumen per square metre.

Illuminance

Where luminance relates to the light produced by a source or reflected by a surface, illuminance describes the light that falls on a surface. We do not see illuminance. What we see is luminance – the light reflected by the surface. The light reflected will be a proportion of the illuminance. A white surface that receives the same illuminance as a black surface will reflect more light and have a greater luminance (or, in visual terms, it will appear brighter). The SI unit for illuminance is lux.

Light meters

A typical light meter measures illuminance – the light falling on a surface. It provides measurements in lux (lumens per square metre), the international SI for illuminance. Illuminance meters are also called lux meters. Some meters also display results in foot-candles, which are widely used in North America. 1 foot-candle = 10.764 lux. To be of use in lighting design, an illuminance meter is calibrated to respond to visible light in a similar fashion to the spectral sensitivity of the human visual system. This calibration is standardized and defined by the CIE (Commission Internationale de l'Eclairage or International Commission on Illumination) photopic sensitivity curve.

As illuminance meters measure the light falling on a surface, they tell us little about the luminous intensity of the surface. For this, a luminance meter is needed. This type of meter is much less common and much more expensive than a lux meter and is rarely used in lighting design.

2. Human factors

When designing lighting, it is important to understand the physics, physiology and psychology of how humans sense light, process it and experience it. This chapter explores how we respond to light, how we adapt to intensity and changes in light levels, and how vision works. Equally important are the psychological aspects of lighting, including mood and cultural preference.

Sensing light

The human body has many ways of understanding its environment. It has a multitude of specialized systems designed to be sensitive to both internal and external changes. Sound and light are two kinds of stimulus that the body is designed to respond to. They are external stimuli and are transmitted through the environment as waves.

Waves can be described in terms of their wavelength (the distance between wave peaks), or by their frequency (the number of wave peaks that pass in a certain period of time). Frequency and wavelength are just different ways of describing the same information about waves. Light is a wave (of electromagnetic energy) that can be described in terms of frequency. Blue light has a frequency of around 660 trillion hertz. However, light is traditionally described in terms of its wavelength rather than its frequency. Blue light is therefore described as having a wavelength of around 470 nanometres (a nanometre is a billionth of a metre).

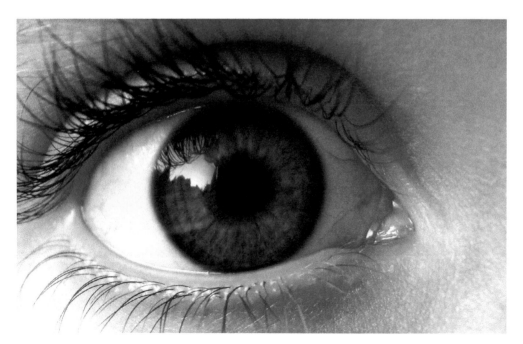

Left
For the lighting designer, sight is the principal means by which the end users will interact with his or her work. It is therefore vital for lighting designers to understand something about how the human eye operates and how it responds to light.

Adaption

Receptors are specialized cells that send signals to the central nervous system when there are changes in the body's internal or external environments. There are different types of receptor for different functions. For example, olfactory receptors respond to the chemical signatures of different odours and trigger our sense of smell, while taste receptors signal flavour to our brains.

All receptors act as transducers, converting one form of energy (for example chemical, mechanical or electromagnetic) into another form that is used to communicate with the brain. Receptors can only be on or off; they have no amplitude or scale of trigger. To communicate the intensity of a signal of a received stimulus (such as the volume of a sound), receptors fire more frequently for a strong stimulus and less frequently for a weaker one.

If a receptor is stimulated for a prolonged time by the same stimulus it begins to decrease its rate of firing, and becomes desensitized to the continuous stimulus. This is called adaption. All receptors display the ability to adapt to a constant stimulus. Walk into a garden and initially the smell of freshly mown grass can be very strong, but it seems to fade even though the smell is still present. When we are adapted to a particular stimulus we only become aware of it again when there is a change: perhaps we go indoors (where we become adapted to the indoor environment), then return to the garden and smell the grass anew. Although we are rarely aware of it, the same process of adaption affects our sense of sight. Our visual system becomes adapted to the colours in our surroundings when we wear tinted sunglasses, and we are surprised at how different the world looks when we remove them.

The process of adaption also allows the visual system to become more sensitive. In a dark space, we become adjusted to lower light levels over a period of time and the space seems to become brighter. During this process of adaption to darkness, the visual system becomes much more sensitive to light, matching its range of sensitivity more closely to the surroundings.

A Optic nerve receptors are stimulated by visible light. The receptors produce a response that is related to the intensity of the stimulus. With a weak stimulus, such as a dim light source being switched on and off, the receptors fire repeatedly for the duration of the stimulus. With a strong stimulus, such as a bright light, the receptors fire more frequently – not more strongly. The visual system can estimate the relative strength of any stimulus by the frequency of receptor signals.

B The optic system is constantly trying to adapt to surrounding conditions. Given the same stimulus after different lengths of time in the dark, the optic nerve receptors fire more frequently as the system becomes more adapted to the darkness. The result is that a light source that seemed weak when seen after only 30 seconds in darkness seems to become brighter the longer the period spent in the dark. Our perception of the brightness of any light stimulus is related to its difference to the background illumination and to our level of adaption to the background illumination. (Illustrations A and B adapted from Gregory, *Eye and Brain: The Psychology of Seeing.*)

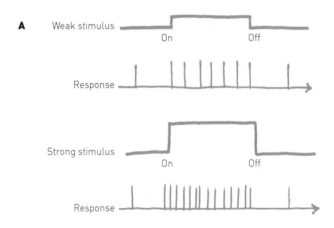

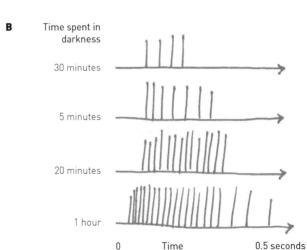

Experiencing changes in light levels

In our built environment there are many times when we encounter rapid changes in the general light level. Moving indoors from the bright sunlight of an outdoor space can leave our eyes struggling to decipher the interior because of the huge drop in relative light levels. The more time we spend in this space, the better adjusted (adapted) we become to its range of light levels. But if we move from what appeared to be a gloomy interior space when we first entered it at midday to a dark night-time scene, we could once again struggle initially with the change in light.

Looking at these examples more closely, there is something interesting going on that can teach us a great deal about our visual system. The difference in illuminance between the sunlit outdoors and the interior space may be something like 50,000 lux outdoors to 500 lux for a (well-lit) interior – a change of some 45,000 lux. Moving from this interior into a night scene illuminated only by street lights may be a move between 500 lux and 5 lux – a change of only 450 lux. On paper, the disparity between a 450,000-lux change and a 450-lux change suggests we will have different levels of difficulty in adapting to the changes. Surely a 450-lux change must be easier to deal with than a 45,000-lux one? However, experience tells us this is not the case.

This illustrates an important feature of our visual system. The rate at which our visual receptors are triggered is a roughly logarithmic response to the light intensity. So, if you wish an object currently illuminated to 100 lux to appear to be twice as bright, you need to increase the light, not by a factor of 2 (to 200 lux), but by a factor of 10 (to 1,000 lux). It is very important to remember this when you are trying to control light for interior spaces, as significant changes in visual brightness require much larger differences in intensity than you may otherwise expect.

A single dim light source added to a sunlit room may make no noticeable difference to the total illumination. However, if the same dim light source is added to a windowless room that contains only one other, dim, light source it can make a very noticeable difference.

Right
The optic nerve receptors do not have a simple 1:1 relationship between the strength of the stimulus and frequency of firing. Instead, the rate of firing has an approximately logarithmic relationship with the stimulus. It will take a ten times increase in stimulus brightness to produce twice as many signals. (Illustration adapted from Gregory, *Eye and Brain: The Psychology of Seeing*.)

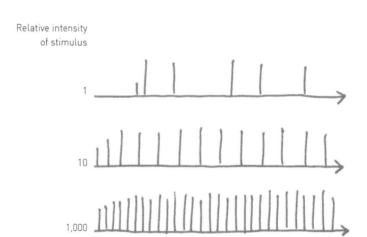

Relative intensity
of stimulus

1

10

1,000

Eyes and the sense of sight

Plants create their own food, relying on chlorophyll, a photosensitive chemical that changes composition on exposure to light. Chlorophyll absorbs the light and provides energy for the process of photosynthesis. Similarly, our sight, and the sight of all seeing animals, relies on a photo pigment. Rhodopsin is a purplish-red pigment contained in the receptor cells in the retina, and its light-reactive qualities have been harnessed to provide the sense of sight by converting the light into a chemical signal to the brain.

To resolve fine detail, a lot of light must be gathered. In turn, this requires quite a large eye. Humans have much larger and more sophisticated eyes than most animals, and sight is one of our most acute senses. The limiting factor in the resolution of an eye is the number of receptors available to capture the incoming light. Human eyes have around 200,000 receptors per square millimetre. By comparison, a hawk may have around 1 million receptors in the same area, which give it its unparalleled ability to identify tiny prey animals from distances far beyond the reach of human vision.

The human eye contains around 120 million receptors, but they are not evenly distributed over the retina. There is one small central part where receptors are very tightly packed. This densely packed area – the fovea – only makes up a tiny part of the surface area of the retina and covers only around 1.5 degrees of our field of view, yet it provides the most detailed part of our vision. Animals whose natural habitat is plains and open country have foveae that are elliptical, stretched horizontally to encompass their surroundings. In contrast, humans have roughly circular foveae that match the eyes of forest-dwelling animals. Our visual system has evolved to deal with the visual complexity of an environment where it was necessary to locate food and danger both horizontally and vertically.

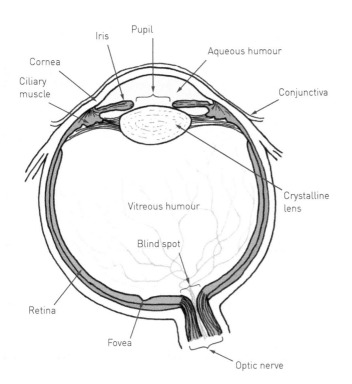

Iris
Pupil
Cornea
Ciliary muscle
Aqueous humour
Conjunctiva
Crystalline lens
Vitreous humour
Blind spot
Retina
Fovea
Optic nerve

Left

The human eye is an amazing confluence of features that collect the light energy that our visual system uses to give us our sense of sight. The muscular contraction of the iris gives some control over the amount of light that can enter the eye, becoming small in very bright conditions and opening up to gather more light in dim conditions. The curve of the front of the eye and the shape of the crystalline lens allows a focused image to be created on the retina at the back of the eye. Muscles around the lens can alter its shape to bring close or distant objects into focus. Light hitting the retina stimulates light-sensitive receptor cells that produce electrical signals, which are sent to the visual cortex in the brain. And yet, as a piece of design, the eye is far from perfect. Limitations include a restricted area of sharp colour vision centred at the fovea; low light sensitivity restricted to the less 'high resolution' parts of the retina; a limited range of iris aperture (which means a limited range of attenuation of bright light); light-sensitive receptor cells positioned behind a net of blood vessels; and an actual hole – a blind spot – in the visual image where the optic nerve exits the back of the eye. Luckily, the visual system can perform remarkable compensations that extend the sensitivity range beyond the physical constraints of the iris. It can produce a full colour image over the whole of our field of view and can even seamlessly fill in our blind spot. The eye is an amazing optical device, but much of the magic of vision happens after light reaches the retina.

Stereo vision

Humans, like other hunting animals, have eyes that are mounted close together on the front of the head, giving a focused, forward-looking view. A large horizontal overlap of around 120 degrees out of a field of view of around 180 degrees gives us acute vision in this main portion of what we can see. The overlapping field of view combined with the spacing between our eyes means our brains receive two slightly different views of a scene, each one offset by the distance between our eyes. Our brain combines the information from the two images and gives us stereo vision – the capacity to accurately estimate the three-dimensional location of an object just by looking at it.

Try looking at an object in the foreground, then shut each eye one at a time. Distant objects will not move much, but one that is close to us will appear to jump significantly between the two views when seen relative to the background. The amount of displacement between the two images is proportional to the distance between our eyes and the object. Our brains can quickly process and decipher this information, to precisely plot the location of objects in three-dimensional space. Stereo vision allows us to accurately pick up objects, or climb and leap onto and over tree branches, and gives us depth perception.

Other optical stimuli can suggest depth without the need for two views. These include overlapping objects, scale, foreshortening and aerial perspective, and are devices employed by painters to give a three-dimensional impression on a two-dimensional surface. An experienced designer can take advantage of these visual cues and use light to manipulate and enhance our visual response to space.

Right
Our eyes are mobile and have a wide potential field of view, but how the eyes are placed within the head restricts how far we can see in any direction. The view from each eye is restricted laterally by the nose and vertically by the brow and cheekbone. When the view from each eye is combined, we get a field of view like this diagram. The dark areas at the top and bottom are where the brow and cheeks obstruct the view. The clear area in the centre is where the coverage of the two eyes overlaps and gives stereo vision. The hatched area is where vision comes from only one eye because of occlusion by the nose.

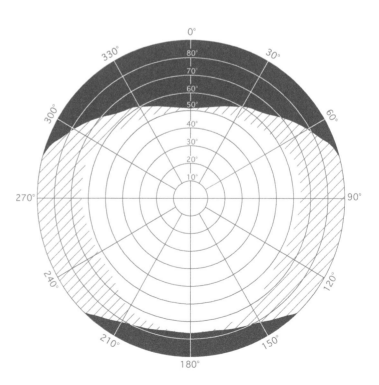

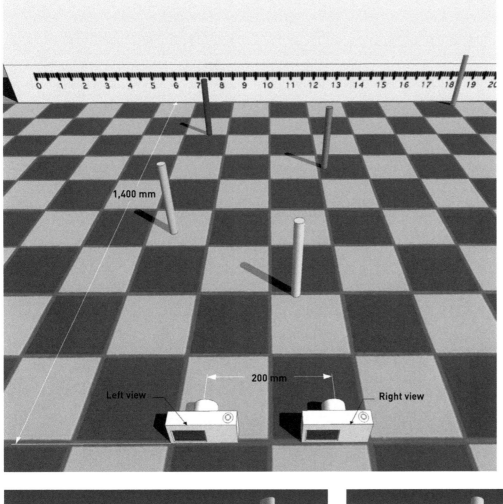

Left
Arrangement of a virtual model illustrating stereo vision. If two cameras (or eyes) are spaced some distance apart and aimed in the same direction, the view each sees will be slightly different.

Below left
The view from the left-hand camera.

Below right
The view from the right-hand camera. Note that the coloured columns obscure the background scale in different locations in each view.

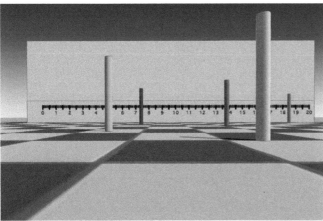

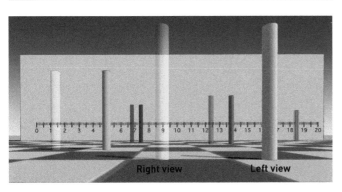

Left
When the left and right images are overlaid it is possible to understand how binocular vision can give depth perception. It is clear from this composite image that the horizontal offset between left and right views of each column is directly related to their distance from the viewer. The yellow column is closest and there is a large gap between the left and right views, while the green columns are furthest away and there is very little offset between the views. Our brains are able to compare the signals from each eye to find areas that match. From the relative offset, the brain can determine the distance to the object.

Motion detection

'All eyes are primarily detectors of movement.'

RICHARD L. GREGORY, *EYE AND BRAIN: THE PSYCHOLOGY OF SEEING*,

SECOND EDITION, 1972, P.94

Even our most acute vision uses receptors that are simple on/off light detectors. Some of these fire only if a light is switched on; some fire only if a light is switched off; others are triggered by a light going on or off. None of them fires with a static state. The receptors are all registering change, and whether this is caused by movement or by lights being switched on and off, the result is still a variation in the amount of light received by the receptor. This is the essence of our vision: it senses change, not stasis. If we could gaze on an unchanging scene without moving our eyes, the scene would begin to fade and we would be unable to 'see' what was in front of us.

If receptors are triggered by movement, what about objects that don't move, such as walls and floors? In a static environment, our movements through the space, turning our head or swivelling our eyes, result in a constantly changing view that, given some contrast in the scene, produces on/off changes that can trigger receptors. Our brain combines this information with physical feedback about our movements and where our eyes are looking to construct a coherent view of the scene.

Even when we feel we are motionless our eyes continue to produce tiny involuntary movements. Called saccadic and micro-saccadic movement, this is totally unconscious. Saccadic movement not only builds a more detailed picture by scanning the very tight cone of our most acute vision over a large area, it also creates apparent motion so that our receptors continue to receive on/off stimuli.

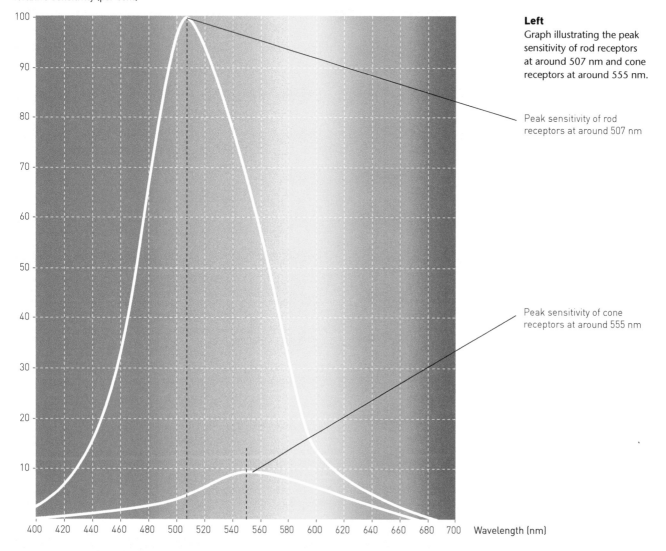

Relative sensitivity (per cent)

Wavelength (nm)

Left
Graph illustrating the peak sensitivity of rod receptors at around 507 nm and cone receptors at around 555 nm.

Peak sensitivity of rod receptors at around 507 nm

Peak sensitivity of cone receptors at around 555 nm

Low light sensitivity

Digital camera sensors and human visual receptors are sensitive instruments: the smallest quantity of light energy, a single photon, is enough to trigger a receptor. But, however sensitive these systems are, they can only detect differences in signals that are above the background level. Unfortunately, even in absolute darkness, there is a small amount of random, accidental firing of receptors. This is described as 'noise'; the signal to noise ratio defines the threshold of sensitivity for any sensing system. The human visual system may be sensitive enough to detect a single photon of light, but a single trigger could easily be caused by random noise. In conditions of very, very low light, our visual system looks for corroboration of the signal by waiting until it receives, in a very short space of time, more triggers from the same receptor or from its neighbours. Only then will the signal be classed as valid and will we be able to 'see' it. However, this system is not perfect. If we stand in a totally dark room, close our eyes and concentrate, after a while we will start to 'see' tiny sparks and flashes in our field of vision. This is noise that the brain is mistakenly interpreting as real incoming light energy.

The human visual system has a strategy for dealing with the different energy levels of daylight and night-time. Colour vision requires a lot of resources in terms of receptors and processing, and it also needs a great deal of light energy. When there is a lot of light around, and the system is not overly burdened by the need to filter random noise, colour vision is a luxury worth having. At night or in low light levels, it is abandoned in favour of very sensitive monochrome vision. The cone receptors, used in high light levels to provide us with colour vision, are abandoned in favour of the much more sensitive rod receptors, which provide us with levels of light and shade. A similar effect is available in some digital video cameras where, in very low light levels, you can switch to 'night shot' mode, which produces a much brighter image at the expense of the colour information.

Top right

This simulated image shows a dark scene with very low contrast, as may be experienced at night. The original image is shown on the right-hand side and random noise is added to the left-hand side. Fine details are lost amid the noise, and only large, bright shapes are still visible. It is easy to see from this demonstration how noise from random firing of our visual receptors can severely degrade the ability of our eyes to resolve fine detail.

Bottom right

The same scene as it may appear in daylight. The left-hand side of the photograph has exactly the same amount of visual noise as the night scene. However, the brighter and higher contrast in the daytime image produces a stronger signal than the noise, and fine details can be seen clearly. Random firing of receptors can happen in daylight, but does not overwhelm the real signals and it is easier for our visual system to filter out the noise.

Light and psychology

The psychology of light and colour is a fascinating subject for anyone with an interest in light, but it is a topic that requires a book in itself. While there is no need to go into great detail here about the psychology of sight, it is worth trying to understand a little about the extent to which psychology influences our sense of sight. This can transform our appreciation of the ways in which we can create beautifully lit environments that generate profound emotional responses in the viewer. Light and colour can produce strong feelings and such a response is not something we want to happen accidentally; we want to be actively in control of the emotional qualities of our lighting designs.

How do we see?

It is tempting to believe that we simply see what is in front of our eyes. But the truth is that we see with our brains, not with our eyes.

Although human beings have many ways of sensing their surroundings, such as touch, hearing, smell, taste and temperature, it is the sense of sight that dominates both our understanding of our world and our descriptions of it. Sight is a very powerful medium that can often override valid information coming from other senses. A 2001 study in France by Morrot, Brochet and Dubourdieu demonstrated the power sight has over people whose expertise is based on their exceptional sense of taste and smell. In the study, professional wine tasters were convinced that a white wine was actually red when a tasteless food colouring was added to it. This was despite the fact that the finely honed sense of smell and taste their livelihood relies on was telling them this was definitely a white wine. So, the visual image of the red liquid overruled the contrary evidence of other senses to convince the tasters that what they saw was the correct interpretation.

This example of wine tasters being fooled by a false sensation shows how the raw data coming from our sense receptors is filtered and interpreted by the brain to give us the final sensation. In the same way, what we see is simply our perception of the scene our eyes are pointed towards, not necessarily the actual scene itself.

There are scores of optical illusions that confuse and deceive us into seeing something that is not there. But almost none of these illusions are optical – within the eye. Instead, they are created by the brain when it applies a false interpretation to the visual information it receives. Our understanding of the world is filtered through our past experiences and knowledge of the world and how it works.

In any scene we turn our gaze on there could be a myriad possible interpretations of the visual information received by our eyes. Two human figures of vastly different sizes could be two people of different physical sizes or they could be a child and an adult. One figure could be close to us and the other far away, the large figure could be real and the other a toy; or the small figure could be real and the large one a photograph on a billboard. The correct interpretation could be any one of these. Rather than presenting us with all these possibilities, the brain uses all available information and experience to filter out impossible or unlikely interpretations.

The visual system has to deal very quickly with a huge amount of information and interpretations can be greatly speeded up if there is heavy weighting towards the ones that are most commonly experienced. For example, a view where a person appears to be transparent is perhaps not as unusual as it sounds. This can happen if there is a transparent reflective surface between the viewer and the person, which can overlay reflections of other objects over the view of the person, making a very complex image. It could also be that the person is reflected in a shop window, but other activities that are visible beyond the window make the person appear to be transparent. However, despite all the film and television effects we may have seen, our brains have never experienced transparent people in real life, so this interpretation is quickly filtered out and we look for explanations based on past experience – such as the fact that glass windows are partially transparent and partially reflective.

Many illusions depend on the brain applying the most likely interpretation based on past experience to an image. In the theatre, an actor can be made transparent by reflecting their image from a very large sheet of glass whose edges are concealed. With no visual clues to indicate that there is a transparent reflective surface on the stage, the only supposedly logical interpretation is that the actor is transparent. Pepper's Ghost (as this technique is known) is an utterly convincing theatrical illusion.

Preferences

Because our sight is influenced by the filter of life experience and the interpretations supplied by the brain, it is very susceptible to bias. Our interpretation of colour also incorporates a vast number of cultural, personal and natural associations. It is important to understand these culturally complex, often contradictory relationships when designing with light and colour.

White is associated with winter, the moon, purity and joy. Despite its impracticality, the white of a doctor's coat suggests cleanliness. A wealth of analogies between colour and natural environments crosses many cultures: blue is the sky and coldness; red is the colour of the sunset, of many fruits and of blood; yellow is the colour of gold and of sunlight – and, as employed by wasps in the natural world, it warns of danger.

Nevertheless, our own cultural experience has a strong influence on associations with colour. In western cultures white represents innocence and is the colour of christening robes and wedding dresses. Yet it was the mourning colour of imperial Rome and nationalist China. For modern Hindus, it represents water, as it did for Ancient Greeks. Black is widely seen as the colour of night and darkness, of disaster and the unknown, yet a black cat crossing your path is a sign of luck in European cultures (and is unlucky in North America). A wedding in Europe or North America is typically white, but would probably be yellow in Hindu culture or red in Chinese cultures. Each culture has a rationale for the symbolism of colour, but this may not match how colours are seen in other cultures.

Colour can also have personal meanings. Orange is the colour of autumn and, in a Buddhist monk's robes, it represents humility. It is the colour of love and happiness in China and Japan, and people who like it are said to be cheerful and quick-witted. As a child, orange was my favourite colour, not for any of these reasons but because it was the best flavour in fruit pastilles. We all have different cultural and personal experiences of light and colour; as designers, we need to be aware that our colour associations may not match those of other people.

Consideration of preferences should not be confined just to strong colours. Even the subtleties of small variations in the colour temperature of white light can be important. This colour temperature is usually described as ranging from red-tinted warm whites through to blue-tinted cool whites. In northern cultures, there is a general preference for warm white light, possibly to recreate the cosy atmosphere of a warming fire. In equatorial regions, where the heat of the midday sun is something to be avoided, the preference is for cool white light, as the blue tint helps to create a subtle feeling of breeziness and coolness.

3. Natural light

This chapter explains the qualities of natural light, including colour and how light is affected by atmospheric conditions. Following this there is a discussion on how to control natural light for human comfort and needs.

What do humans need?

Geneticists believe that all the humans currently living are descended from about 600 individuals. Around 164,000 years ago, a progenitor population of the modern human lived in coastal caves in South Africa's Western Cape (Pinnacle Point caves). The appearance of *Homo sapiens* is the most recent stage in more than 5 million years of human evolution. Until very recently, our species has evolved in an environment dominated by patterns of natural light.

It is difficult, in the world of modern humans, to imagine a world without controllable light sources. Electric light has always been a part of the world in our lifetime, and it is easy to think that it is normal. However, the incandescent lamp has only existed for around 100 years and we have had controllable electric lighting for only 0.06 per cent of the time since our ancestors lived on the southern coast of Africa, or less than 0.002 per cent of human evolution.

Below
Our long affinity with sunlight is embodied in this depiction of a man and the sun in a 12,000-year-old Brazilian cave painting.

We have had thousands of millennia to evolve our complex interaction with, and dependence on, the most available light source: natural light. By comparison, we quickly became accustomed to electric light in the last century. Despite our incredible adaptability, evolution has physically and mentally equipped humans for life in a naturally lit world. Understanding this can allow us to create lit environments that feel comfortable, appear natural and are physically and mentally good for us. We also have the means to deliberately or accidentally create uncomfortable and unhealthy environments by working against natural light patterns. In this sense, the designer has enormous power to influence not only visual perception, but also the emotional and physical experience of the built environment. To be able to do this intentionally, we need to understand the patterns and qualities of natural light.

Above left
The lives of our ancestors were governed by the rhythm of natural light, its movement, direction, intensity, colour, day and night.

Above right
Electric light has allowed us to create 24-hour buildings that never sleep. Barajas Airport, Madrid, Spain.

Sources of natural light

The natural world contains several sources of light that have not been created by humans, such as fire, lightning and even bioluminescence from deep-sea creatures and fireflies. But when we talk about natural light, we really mean daylight.

Sunlight is an incredible resource for our planet. Without it, there would be no life. Sunlight has illuminated the earth for millennia and as 'the light of life' it is the light in which humans have evolved to operate best. The human visual system and our psychological and physiological response to light and colour is intrinsically related to daylight and its essential qualities.

Either directly or indirectly, the light of the sun is our planet's dominant natural light source. Sunlight reaches the earth in several forms as direct light from the sun, reflected and diffused by clouds, scattered in the upper atmosphere to create the blue sky or reflected from objects on the surface of the planet.

The visible light that leaves the sun is a very cool white light with a colour temperature of around 6,000 kelvin. As sunlight approaches the earth, it is scattered by tiny particles in the upper atmosphere. This process, called Rayleigh scattering, scatters blue light most strongly while transmitting more light of other wavelengths. The result is that a lot of the sun's blue light is scattered in the atmosphere, which gives the sky its blue colour. Because of this scattering, the direct sunlight that reaches the surface

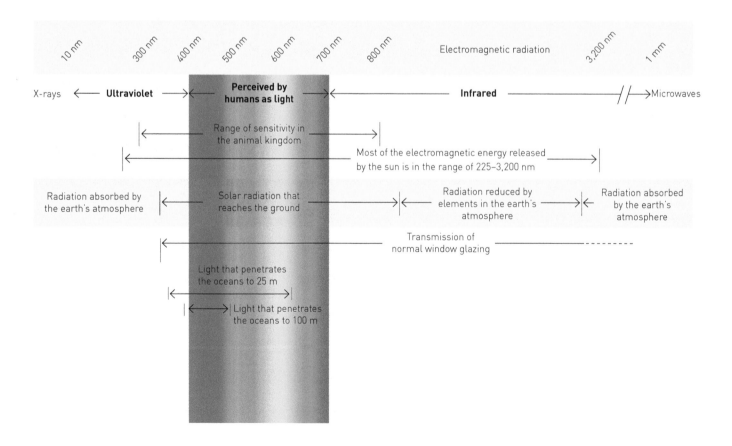

of the earth is much warmer in colour appearance than it would otherwise be. However, the combination of a slightly yellower sun with strong blue from the sky means that average daylight on the earth has a very similar colour temperature to the natural white light from the sun itself.

Sunlight is also scattered by water and ice in the atmosphere, but because of the much larger size of water droplets in clouds all wavelengths of light are scattered and the light retains its white colour. Although all but the darkest storm clouds still transmit large amounts of light, the scattering can create a very diffuse quality of light. Even on completely overcast days, when there is no visible sunlight, illumination levels can be high. But there is still something dispiriting about an overcast day. We describe it as dull, and the atmosphere it creates can be depressive and ominous.

Many features of an overcast sky are best avoided in interior lighting if we do not want to create depressive environments. The most obvious one is the almost uniform and directionless quality of the light. With no direction, we can lose the visual trigger for which way is up. The lack of shadows means we have lost one of the more subtle visual clues to three-dimensional shape and texture.

Less immediately obvious is the change in colour temperature. From an average of 6,500 kelvin for daylight (depending greatly on weather conditions and where you are in the world), an overcast sky can cast a very cool white light of around 10,000 kelvin. This has a strong association with bad weather, and, in interior spaces, when it is combined with uniform illuminance and no directional light the depressive effect can be as strong as it would be outdoors.

It is always worth comparing a proposed lighting approach to natural lighting conditions – after all, this is exactly what our visual system does when we are presented with these conditions. Whether we are aware of it or not, we are always comparing interior lighting with our experience of exterior lighting.

Right
A snowy hillside is the perfect place to see just how much of the light at ground level is contributed by the sky. The low angle of sunlight in this image throws much of the slope into shadow. The shadow is not black because it is still receiving direct light from the sky – hence the strong blue tint to the shadows.

Below

Even in the shade, on a sunny day there is a lot of ambient light around – 12,400 lux in the measurement shown on the left. Nevertheless, this figure is less than one-seventh of the 87,100 lux measured from the direct sunlight on the right. A 7:1 variation in light levels over such a small distance would normally be designed out of the lighting of an interior space, yet this extreme contrast is exactly what natural light is all about.

Range of intensity

Compared to our experience of electric light, natural light has a wide range of levels, even over the course of a few hours. Indoors, we typically experience illumination levels over a range of around 1,000:1 (the brightest object to the dimmest object we may encounter). By contrast, a 12-hour period of natural light, from midday to midnight, could provide more than a 1 million:1 range of illumination. This relatively huge range of intensities is a defining feature of natural light and is what our visual system has evolved to cope with.

The daily variation in light levels is also accompanied by an annual cycle. Because of the axial tilt of the earth, there are very few parts of the world that do not exhibit noticeable seasonal variations in natural light. The further from the equator, the more pronounced the seasonal variation. London is around 51 degrees north of the equator and has a temperate climate. Because of the relative tilt towards the sun in summer and the tilt away from it in winter, there is a distinct difference between day lengths in summer and winter. The earth's tilt is also reflected in the differing quantities of available light that reaches its surface at different times of the year. At midday, an average overcast sky with no direct sunlight can produce around 35,000 lux at ground level in summer, but only a fifth of that in winter.

Direction of natural light

The principal direction of natural light is from overhead. The combination of direct sunlight and diffused sky light produces a very strong downward direction to natural light. However, the reason we can see green plants or rocky hills around us is because they are reflecting light towards us. The direct light from above is much stronger than light reflected off surfaces at ground level, but the reflected light can provide a significant amount of ambient light. However, even in the shadiest conditions, the brightest areas tend to be above us. This feature of daylight is one element that can make a particular direction of light feel natural or not.

A very strong uplight illuminating a person has an unnatural quality, partly because it is not seen as a natural direction for light. Of course, it is not impossible to have that situation replicated in the real world. Sunlight reflected from a reflective surface such as water or a smooth wet rock can produce intense uplighting. However, this situation is rare enough for the brain to apply its experience filter to any uplit scene and class it as an unnatural light direction.

Above
Even in deeply shaded areas, the norm is for the brightest part of a view to be above us.

Left
Although a completely overcast sky with total cloud cover can look as though it is completely uniform, there can be significant variations. The average luminance of a totally overcast sky is around 42° above the horizon. At 5° above the horizon the sky has only half the luminosity of the average. The zenith light from directly overhead can be 30% brighter than the average. This variation in sky luminance can be important when designing glazing systems. Even on overcast days, roof glazing that allows in zenith light could allow in around 2½ times as much natural light per square metre of opening compared to vertical glazing that only allows in near-horizontal light.

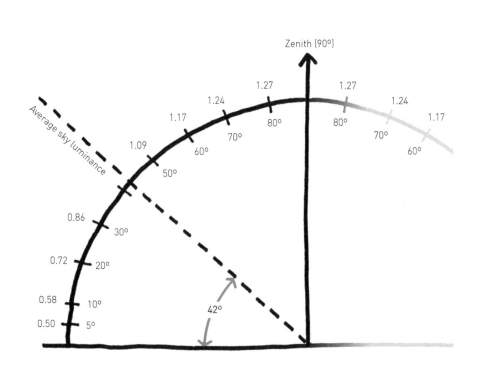

COLOUR AND NATURAL LIGHT

Over the course of a day, there is a large fluctuation in the colour of natural light. We are very aware of the changes from sunrise to midday to sunset, but there is a more subtle but constant variation throughout the whole day. There is a qualitative difference between morning light and afternoon light that goes beyond the change of the sun's position in the sky.

The changes may take place too slowly for us to be aware of the slight colour shift, but they are there nonetheless and the quality of natural light can supply us with an intuitive awareness of the time of day.

1 Rayleigh scattering in the upper atmosphere scatters blue light most strongly, giving us the blue sky, a feature that we associate most with clear skies and bright sunlight in the middle of the day.

2 Light can also be scattered by dust and pollen in the lower atmosphere. As with scattering in the upper atmosphere, blue light is affected most strongly, leading to the familiar blue mist that sometimes obscures distant mountains. Artists call this effect 'aerial perspective' and it can be a strong visible signifier of distance in the natural world.

3 Even on overcast days, there can be a remarkable range of colours on display in the sky.

4 Before the sun begins to set it often takes on a subtle golden quality.

5 While Rayleigh scattering affects blue light most strongly, it scatters all the colours of visible light. The light from the setting sun has to travel through much more atmosphere than the overhead light at midday. By the time its light has reached the viewer, all the blue light has been scattered, leaving sunlight that gets progressively redder as the sun sinks below the horizon.

6 After the sun has set, natural light is still provided by the sky and clouds. The very high-level clouds in the top right of this image are illuminated by sunlight. There is a definite shift towards a cool blue light in these conditions.

7 Even on a cloudy night there is still some light in the sky, and a long-exposure photograph can capture its dusky blue quality two hours after the sun has set.

8 For interior spaces, the direction in which glazing faces has an impact on the colour quality of the natural light that enters a space. In this image, the warm light of an early-morning sun enters through an east-facing window and illuminates the wall around the picture. The left-hand side of the wall is only illuminated by the very cool light of a north-facing window. While this is an extreme example, window placement should take into account the colour quality of light from different directions.

Left
We can use our experience of the natural world to estimate the time of day and time of year at which a photograph was taken. Although the sun is not visible in this image, it is clear from the deep shadows that it is low in the sky to the right of the frame. Normally, the sun being so low in the sky would suggest a time either shortly after sunrise or just before sunset. Yet the quality of light seems to be neither early nor late in the day. The colour is wrong: at sunrise or sunset the light would have an obvious warm colour tint. Therefore, the most logical answer is that the photograph was taken in winter, when the sun can be low in the sky while still retaining a cool white light. This kind of assessment of natural light is an innate human ability that allows us to make these kinds of judgements very quickly without even being aware that we are making them. We are constantly applying our knowledge and past experience of natural lighting conditions to make judgements about what we are seeing.

Below left
This gallery in the Musée d'Orsay, Paris, by ACT Architecture Group, is toplit with natural light from a skylight. The light is controlled by a square louvre at a high level with deep baffles at a lower level that prevent any direct light hitting the sensitive artworks. The resulting light in the gallery is reflected from several surfaces to produce an even spread of light across the display surfaces. Even during daylight hours, the natural light is backed up with electric light from luminaires mounted in the top of the deep baffles. The addition of electric light in this situation allows for a relatively constant illumination level to be maintained by tracking the available daylight, and dimming or increasing the electric light in response.

Below right
Cathedral architecture is all about mastering the control of natural light. High-level clerestory glazing allows direct light into the building from a celestial high angle. Meanwhile, light at low level is filtered through stained glass to infuse the interior with colour.

Daylight control

The range of colour, direction and illuminance available from daylight is incomparable. It often brings great joy and interest to our experience of the outside world, yet it can be problematic for many interiors. Leaving aside the thermal issues caused by excessive sunlight penetration into building interiors, the huge range of light levels and contrast in the outside world can cause real problems if replicated inside.

Daylight control for interior spaces can take many forms. In some climates it is about reducing excessive light and heat, and in others it is about maximizing the amount of natural light and warmth. But control of daylight can also be a celebration of the qualities of natural light. There is a great lineage of architecture that has been designed to capture its particular effects. Consider prehistoric structures such as Stonehenge in England, which is aligned to the light of the sun at particular times of the year; the open oculus of the Pantheon in Rome, which allows a single patch of sunlight to trace its apparent daily movement across the interior walls of the building, or the work of contemporary architects such as Steven Holl (see below).

TIP USING SIMPLE MODELS

Full daylight modelling is a complex task, but even simple card models can help us to understand how sunlight penetration is affected by different sizes and shapes of vertical glazing and roof glazing, and by different room proportions.

Top left
In the Pantheon in Rome, daylight enters through a circular opening at the apex of the dome. The circular patch of sunlight tracks over the interior surface as the day progresses, giving a clear indication of the passage of time.

Top right and bottom left and right
The careful control of daylight is a distinguishing feature of the work of architect Steven Holl. The Chapel of St Ignatius at Seattle University contains a host of architectural devices designed to capture and mould the changing daylight, to produce special moments of magic for the congregation. This is daylight design at the highest level, yet it follows a long line of sophisticated architectural manipulation of natural light.

Case study Architecture Gallery, Victoria & Albert Museum, London, UK

Lighting Design Speirs And Major Associates

January 21, 12pm

February 21, 12pm

March 21, 12pm

April 21, 12pm

May 21, 12pm

June 21, 12pm

Light is energy and exposure to high levels of light can alter the chemical constitution and degrade many materials. It is a particular concern in the museum and gallery world, where restricted light levels are used to protect precious exhibits. It is a challenge to design the lighting for any exhibition that contains exhibits that need to be displayed in restricted light levels far below average daylight levels. It is especially difficult when the exhibition space has tall, south-facing windows in a preserved historic building that cannot be altered from the outside.

The Architecture Gallery at the Victoria & Albert Museum in London presented all these problems along with the additional wish from the client and the heritage organization that the glazing should not simply be blacked out and that visitors could still see out of the building.

From initial calculations, it was clear to the lighting designers that, with such a large amount of glazing, even an overcast sky would be likely to produce average daylight levels in the room that were 20 times the maximum allowed for some exhibits. The amount of light energy contained in a single hour of unfiltered direct sunlight entering this gallery could exceed the maximum exposure recommended for a whole year. An effective solution had to be found.

The daylight control solution chosen for this gallery does not rely on a single method to control the daylight, but a layered approach. Direct sunlight is controlled with an internal micro-louvre and by careful positioning of the display structures. As ultraviolet is the most damaging part of the spectrum, specialist window films are used on the glazing to cut out the UV component of the daylight. Another film reduces the light levels without colouring the light, while louvres and translucent banners further reduce the natural light to manageable levels.

The daylight control solutions were designed with the use of computer modelling to track the movement of sunlight over the course of a year and calculations of the daylight levels that could be expected inside the gallery.

Above
When designing the lighting for a gallery refurbishment at the Victoria & Albert Museum in London, designers Speirs and Major Associates used modelling software to track the pattern of direct sunlight that would enter the space through the large south-facing windows at different times of the year. In a gallery environment, direct sunlight can be very damaging to exhibits and must be tightly controlled. This sun-path study allowed the designers to assess various structural options within the space to see how they would affect the pattern of daylight in the gallery.

62°
— Centre point of window

$$\text{Average daylight factor} = \frac{T \times W \times \emptyset \times MF}{A\,(I - R^2)}\ \%$$

50 metres across street to adjacent buildings

Above
Daylighting calculations do not have to involve lots of computer work. This illustration shows the hand-calculated daylight factor formula used by Speirs and Major Associates to estimate the amount of natural light that south-facing gallery space would expect to receive.

Above left
The daylight-control solution chosen by the lighting designers involved several mechanisms to reduce the daylight to manageable levels. The glazing has a tinted film applied that reduces the incoming light and eliminates the ultraviolet component of the incoming daylight, as UV light is especially damaging to sensitive museum exhibits. There is also a woven architectural micro-louvre system applied to the inside of the window frames. Arranged like a miniature venetian blind, this system prevents high-angle sunlight entering the room while allowing views out at low angles. The result is clear in this image, where trees can be seen outside but the upper part of the window appears dark – as all light is natural, light from high angles is excluded. The louvre system is not really obvious to gallery visitors from normal viewing positions.

Above right
The daylight control for the Architecture Gallery was completed with a printed translucent banner over the window. The banner solution was suggested by the lighting designers, Speirs and Major Associates, for areas with particularly light-sensitive exhibits. It allows some variation in the natural light entering the gallery, but reduces the total daylight illumination enough to allow the exhibits to be picked out from their background with spotlights.

4. Electric light

This chapter explains aspects of electric light from the different sources, to types of luminaire (light fixtures) and their effects, to designing patterns and controlling light.

Below
A modern city without electric light is almost inconceivable. Used for illumination, for signage and for decoration, electric light extends our active day beyond the daylight hours.

Sources of electric light

There are many specialist niche products in the lighting industry, but in architectural lighting there are three principal lighting technologies we are likely to encounter. Incandescent sources produce visible light by heating a material (usually a thin metal filament). They include traditional incandescent lamps, and tungsten halogen, low-voltage tungsten halogen and tungsten xenon lamps. Discharge light sources produce light by creating an electrical discharge through a gas. They include fluorescent lamps, and metal halide and sodium lamps. Electroluminescent light sources include electroluminescent panels, light-emitting diodes (LEDs), and organic LEDs (OLEDs).

Incandescent light sources

Hot things radiate energy: the hotter they are, the more energy they radiate. Hot materials that radiate heat are producing infrared radiation. Infrared radiation is part of the electromagnetic spectrum, and in terms of radiant power it sits just below the visible light spectrum. If a hot object gets even hotter, it will radiate more electromagnetic energy and will eventually produce light as well as heat. The material has become *incandescent*.

An increase in the heat of the incandescent material is accompanied by a change in the wavelengths of light that are produced. Incandescent materials produce mostly heat (infrared energy). As they get hotter, they begin to produce red light, then each colour of the spectrum is added as the energy levels increase until the incandescent material produces all the colours of the spectrum and becomes white hot.

Fire is one of the most familiar instances of incandescence – combustible materials become so hot they burst into flames and release energy as both heat and light.

Above
The glowing embers of a wood fire produce mostly heat, but they also radiate light. The embers have become incandescent and produce light of a colour that represents their surface temperature. The parts of this fire that are 'red hot' are cooler than the parts that are producing orange, yellow or white light.

Below
The thin tungsten filament in this incandescent lamp heats up as electrical energy flows through it. With no electrical energy, the filament is cold and dark. As the electrical energy increases, the filament heats up and radiates electromagnetic energy in the form of heat. As the energy levels increase, the filament becomes so hot it begins to radiate visible light as well as heat energy. The light produced is mostly around the red end of the spectrum – it is red hot. Further increases in energy input result in more, higher-power electromagnetic energy being produced; orange, yellow, green and then blue wavelengths are added to the red light. Eventually the filament radiates all the colours of visible light – it has become white hot. The colour of the light produced by the filament is directly related to its temperature.

Discharge light sources

An electric current passing through a gas can produce visible light. This is a completely different process to the way incandescent sources produce light. The excitation of the gas by the electricity causes collisions between atoms and these collisions result in the release of energy in the form of ultraviolet or visible light. In the natural world, the most common electrical discharge we experience is lightning – lightning is an electrical discharge through air. It lasts only for a short time, but it produces a very intense flash of visible light.

As the gas discharge process does not involve heating materials as with incandescent light sources, it is generally a much more efficient way of producing visible light. Gas discharge lamps can offer a much longer life than most incandescent sources. Combined with their greater efficiency, this makes them an attractive alternative to incandescent lamps in many situations.

Creating a gas discharge that produces visible light is a much more involved process than the relatively simple heating of an incandescent filament. It requires a lot of energy to start the discharge in the first place, and the energy flow then has to be reduced and controlled very precisely to maintain a steady discharge. This means complex electrical control devices are needed to operate discharge lamps. The devices are commonly called ballasts or control gear.

There are many different kinds of discharge lamp. They have a wide range of functions, from general lighting to producing coloured light or being used in tanning booths. The different types contain different combinations of gas and additives such as metallic compounds. Commonly used gases include helium, neon, argon, xenon, krypton and nitrogen. The gases are often combined with small amounts of metals such as sodium and mercury. When activated by an electrical discharge, the different gases and combinations of materials produce radiation in different parts of the spectrum. This means different colours of visible light can be produced by different gases/metal halides. By combining the gases, the different colours can be mixed to produce a whiter light source.

Discharge light sources are more efficient than incandescent sources because they produce more visible light for the energy used. However, they are most efficient at higher wattages, and it is difficult to produce very low-power discharge lamps that have high efficiency.

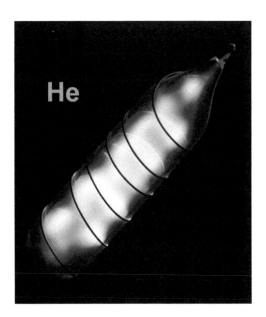
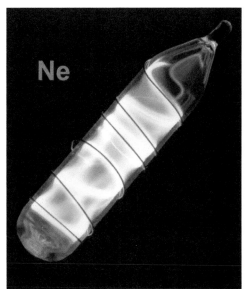
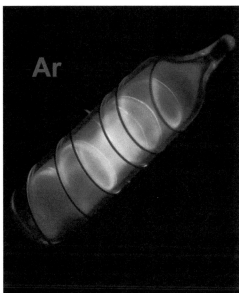
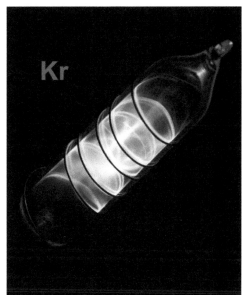
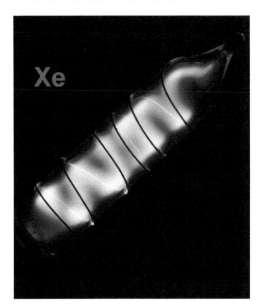

Left
When an electrical discharge is passed through different gases, they produce visible radiation in different parts of the spectrum. Helium (He) produces a very pink light while neon (Ne) produces an orange-red light that is characteristic of classic American motel and bar signs. Argon (Ar) is one of the most commonly used gases in cold cathode lamps and naturally produces a purple-blue glow. Krypton (Kr) creates a bright white light. Xenon (Xe) is one of the rarest elements on earth; it produces a very intense bluish white light and is often used in automobile headlight lamps.

Low Pressure Discharge Lamps operate at internal pressures lower than atmospheric pressure – the lamp is a partial or total vacuum. They include fluorescent lamps (compact fluorescent lamps are essentially the same as straight linear ones, except they are twisted and coiled to fit a smaller space); cold cathode lamps (typically used for signage, these are commonly known as neon lamps, though this is erroneous as they often contain argon and not neon gas); and sodium lamps (these produce a very orange light and are most commonly used for street lighting).

Fluorescent lamps are perhaps the most common modern light source. They come in a range of physical shapes and sizes, different wattages and different colours – though usually some form of white. At its heart, a fluorescent lamp is actually producing ultraviolet radiation, not visible light. The white coating that we see on the inside of the glass tube is a layer of phosphors and minerals that react to UV radiation. The phosphors absorb the high-energy UV radiation and reradiate some of it as lower-energy visible light. This process is called fluorescence. Fluorescent lamps can be produced in a wide range of tints of white. A different mix of phosphors is used to create each different tint.

Right
A standard CD can be used as a simple spectroscope. When seen reflected in a CD, the light from a low-voltage tungsten halogen spotlight (top) and compact fluorescent lamp (bottom) is diffracted by the fine grooves in the CD's surface, splitting the white light into its component colours. The low-voltage tungsten halogen lamp is an incandescent light source; the white light it produces contains all the colours of the spectrum. By contrast, the typical low-wattage compact fluorescent lamp has a very broken spectrum. It produces white light, but there are large gaps in its spectral output. This means that although its light appears white, some colours will not be rendered correctly by this light source.

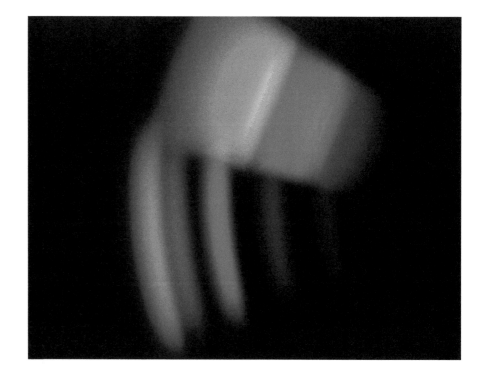

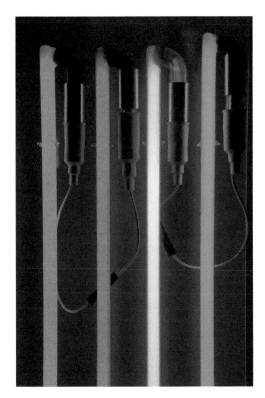

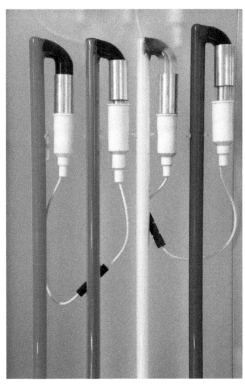

Left

Cold cathode lamps are discharge light sources similar to fluorescent lamps. While fluorescent lamps are produced almost exclusively in white colours, cold cathode lamps are made in a large range of colours and tints of white. The colours can be produced by using different gases in the tube (neon gas glows red, argon glows blue); phosphor coatings can be used to modify the output of a blue or ultraviolet discharge; coloured glass can further modify the light produced. By combining these techniques, the manufacturer of these cold cathode tubes has a range of around 55 different colours. In the sample colour set shown here, the valentine red, shocking pink, electric blue and sea green lamps look quite different when switched off. Although neon-filled tubes are the best-known reds, all the lamps in this set use argon. The red and green tubes at each end use phosphors and coloured glass, while the pink and blue ones use only phosphors to create the colours.

Left

With discharge lamps that produce white light with the aid of phosphor coatings, such as fluorescent lamps and the white cold cathode lamps illustrated here, different combinations of phosphors can create different tints of white light. In this example, the three white, cold cathode lamps contain phosphor mixes designed to match the quality of white light available from incandescent light sources operating at 4,200 K, 3,500 K and 3,000 K. In the left-hand image, the colours are boosted for printing purposes, but when the lamps are seen in real life, it is clear that the 4,200 K lamp on the left is bluer than the warm white of the 3,000 K lamp on the right. The second image has no colour boost, but the exposure was reduced to demonstrate the subtlety of the colour tints.

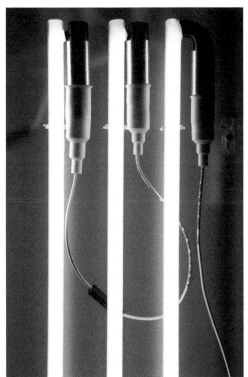

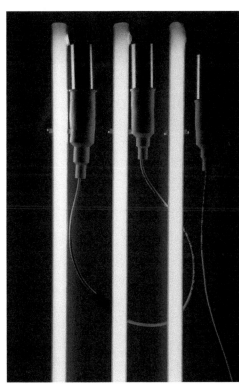

Above
These luminaires use 400 W high-intensity discharge lamps to create a daylight quality in a perimeter void for an office building. The camera is less tolerant of colour tints in white light than the human visual system: where the camera records a distinct green tinge to the lamps, the eye sees something closer to cool white daylight at 6,500 K.

High-intensity discharge lamps operate with an internal pressure greater than atmospheric pressure. They include high-pressure sodium lamps (used for street lighting, these produce an orange light that is slightly whiter than that created by low-pressure sodium lamps); metal halide lamps (a wide-ranging category of lamps that produce anything from low-quality whitish light through to very high-quality white light); and mercury vapour lamps (a relatively old technology that produces a slightly green form of white light).

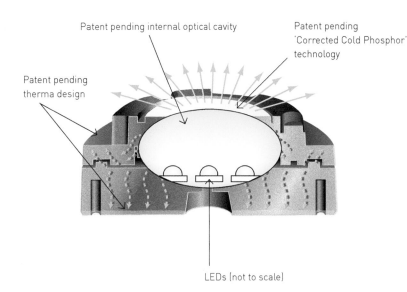

Patent pending internal optical cavity

Patent pending
'Corrected Cold Phosphor'
technology

Patent pending
therma design

LEDs (not to scale)

Electroluminescent light sources

Electroluminescent (EL) materials produce electromagnetic radiation (usually visible light) in response to an electric current. Unlike incandescence, this process does not require the application of heat, so electroluminescent light sources are inherently cooler. They also do not rely on the creation of an electric discharge through a gas, so they can be physically much smaller than discharge light sources. Many electroluminescent light sources are very low power, but also have correspondingly low brightness. Many mobile phones, MP3 players and vehicle instrument panels use electroluminescent panels to backlight the display. The thin and flat electroluminescent film is ideal for this purpose, but it does not produce enough light for general lighting use. The process of light production in a light-emitting diode (LED) also operates on the electroluminescent principle, but LEDs can be made as higher-power devices that can produce much more light.

LEDs represent one of the most recent advances in lighting technology. Although LEDs themselves have existed since the 1930s, it was the late 1990s before a practical, high-brightness, blue LED existed that allowed full colour mixing using red, green and blue devices. Although RGB-based light sources are capable of producing an approximation of white light, modern white light LEDs operate in a similar way to fluorescent lamps. The LED light source itself produces ultraviolet or near-ultraviolet light and this excites a phosphor coating that, in turn, produces visible white light. This process has, at last, allowed the creation of reliable and efficient white light LED light sources that are suitable for general use in architectural lighting.

Although LEDs are widely known as being super-efficient light sources, such claims have often been

Above left
High-quality white light LED light sources do not produce the white light directly, nor do they mix the light from red, green and blue LEDs. They consist of a LED module that contains several LEDs that produce near-ultraviolet light; the individual LED chips are sealed in a chamber below a cover glass that is coated with phosphors (the yellow area in this image). The phosphors react to the ultraviolet radiation and produce visible light. A combination of different phosphors is used to create the desired colour temperature of white light. The precise quantity of each phosphor is controlled accurately to ensure very high levels of colour consistency between modules. This level of colour accuracy and colour quality exists only at the top end of the LED market.

Above right
This drawing, by the manufacturer, shows a section through an Xicato white LED module. The LED light sources are bonded onto a heat sink to pull heat away from the sensitive devices. The sources sit within an optical chamber that concentrates the ultraviolet light onto the cover glass, which has a coating of phosphors. The coating fluoresces and produces visible white light from the module.

exaggerated. Until very recently, high-quality white light LEDs used in real-life situations were only as efficient as a good-quality, low-voltage tungsten halogen lamp. However, lamp efficacy is only a very small part of quantifying how effective a lighting installation is at producing usable light from the power it consumes: an efficient lamp does not directly result in an efficient lighting scheme. While the core LED technology was not ultra-efficient at producing visible light, the very small physical size of the light source allowed for the creation of optical devices to gather and direct the light that were much more accurate than could be easily achieved with any other light source. The result was that much more of the light produced by the source could be directed where the user wanted it to go.

LED efficiency increases every year, but it could still be some time before ultra-efficient LED sources that outperform the best fluorescent and discharge lamps graduate from laboratory prototypes into real-life, usable luminaires. Nevertheless, this relatively low-power and low-heat light source is likely to become the dominant white light source in most areas of general lighting.

Organic Light Emitting Diodes (OLEDs) are a new area of lighting technology that promises to combine the advantages of EL panels (thin, flexible sheets of light-emitting material) with the higher light output of LED devices. OLEDs are a technology that still requires a lot of development, and as light sources, they are unlike anything people are used to working with. OLEDs represent a luminous surface rather than the luminous points that traditional luminaires and optical systems are designed around.

Right
The small size of LED light sources can allow the creation of luminaires that are physically tiny compared to traditional lamp and luminaire combinations. The linear luminaire shown here incorporates a strip of warm white LED sources. The luminaire body has a cross section of only 16.5 mm wide by 12 mm tall.

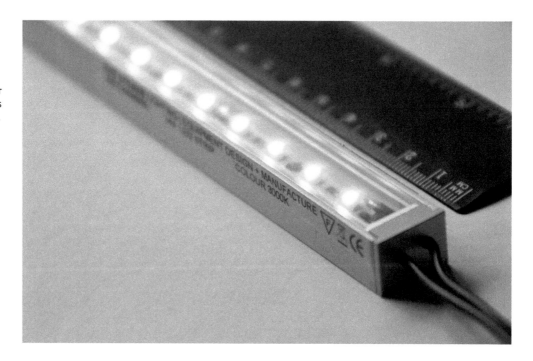

Luminaires

Many words are used to describe lighting equipment; for example, in domestic settings, the word 'lamp' is often used, as in 'table lamp' or 'floor lamp'. For a professional, a lamp is the light source itself and the word is not used to describe anything else. The word 'light' is also often used in contexts like 'ceiling light' or 'desk light'. For a professional, this is also inappropriate: light is what the equipment should produce, not what it is called. The phrase 'light fitting' is perhaps the best term for a non-technical person to use, as it describes the function of the equipment and that it is some kind of assemblage. In fact, light fitting is widely used in theatrical situations to describe lighting equipment.

However, the technically correct term is 'luminaire'. Although a computer spell-checker is unlikely to recognize the word, it is the only one that describes what we mean when we talk about lighting equipment. A luminaire is a complete package that includes light source, lamp holder, reflector, lenses, housing, suspension, mounting, and so on – everything that goes to make the complete light fitting. Luminaire is the word most widely used in architectural lighting, and it is the one we shall adopt when talking about lighting equipment. However, when talking to non-specialists, luminaires can best be described as light fittings.

Although novels are made from combinations of only 26 letters, 10 digits and some punctuation, how these are combined and recombined can create incredible complexity. From very simple components, wondrous tales can be woven. The skill of a great author is not in knowing all the words, but in knowing when to use them.

At its core, lighting design also has just a few simple components. It is the skill involved in combining these components and how they are positioned that creates the beautiful narrative of a great lighting scheme. The lighting designer must be selective in choosing the lit effects and lighting equipment that will deliver the design he or she has envisioned. No matter what science and technology is involved, remember that there are only a few generic luminaire types and that successful lighting projects rely on the intelligent application of simple principles. It is easy to be blinded by the technology involved in many luminaires, but it is not the technology that creates great lighting – the designer does.

Dispersive and directional luminaires

The quality of light in a space is more than just a function of the luminaires; it is also dependent on their positioning and use. A linear fluorescent lamp located in a narrow ceiling slot can produce a directional quality of light, while a narrow spotlight positioned to reflect light off a white wall can produce a soft and diffused quality of light. Dispersive luminaires spread their light over a wide area with no defined direction to the flow of light.

Dispersive luminaires may use materials such as frosted glass or fabric shades to diffuse the light. Or they may simply rely on the natural diffuse effect of light sources such as linear or compact fluorescent lamps. The characteristics of a dispersive or diffused light source include a lack of shadows or a distinct softness to any shadows, with the luminaire illuminating surfaces all around it. In a typical light-coloured room, a bare lamp can often provide this quality of light as it reflects off the various surfaces.

Where we want to aim the light, we may use a directional luminaire, designed to do the opposite of a dispersive one. Directional luminaires control the spread of light to give it a real directional quality. This may be done by using simple shades and baffles or highly technical polished reflectors and lenses. Some light sources, such as dichroic spotlights, come ready packaged with a reflector to control the spread of light, and many LED light sources come bonded to a specially designed plastic lens to create a controlled beam of light.

It is important to remember that the energy efficiency of a lighting scheme cannot be simply a measure of how efficient any particular light source is at producing visible light. It must take into account the quality of the luminaire and even how the luminaire will be used. Almost all the light sources you are likely to come across will naturally produce a wide spread of light. It is the reflection of light from polished surfaces or the refraction of light through transparent lenses that creates the defined beam of a directional luminaire. The reflection and refraction process is never 100 per cent efficient, so the quality of the reflectors or lenses can make a significant difference to the ability of a luminaire to convert the uncontrolled light from the light source into useful directional light. This is described as the light output ratio (LOR). While a bare, fluorescent batten luminaire could have an LOR of 99 per cent, a typical high-quality downlight luminaire for compact fluorescent lamps could have an LOR of 45 per cent. This means more than half the light energy being produced by the light source does not make it out of the luminaire as usable light. It sounds as though the downlight is a terrible waste of energy, but all its output is within a tightly controlled spread, and can illuminate the surfaces below it to a much higher level than a bare lamp that spreads light in all directions.

Concealed luminaires

When it comes to working with light, luminaires are not the end of the design process. The designer needs to remember that selecting a luminaire is not the same as designing the lighting for a space. Choice of light source and choice of generic luminaire type are just part of the lit effect of a space. Another vital component is how the luminaires will be used within the space. A luminaire has a physical presence and it is easy to focus on the aesthetics of what it looks like rather than what it actually does to enhance the lit environment. Simple or aesthetically unattractive luminaires can produce beautiful lit effects if they are used in the correct way. Where the lit effect takes precedence over the visible aesthetics of the lighting equipment, concealed luminaires can be the ugliest objects imaginable provided they produce the desired effect.

Manufacturer's data

Reading and deciphering the photometric data about luminaires is often a minefield for the uninitiated. The issue can often be confused by the way in which the photometric data is presented. Gross oversimplification of photometric diagrams is one problem, but the data supplied is frequently presented as seemingly impenetrable graphs, charts and numbers. The more we are able to understand the manufacturer's photometric data, the better able we will be to visualize the lit effect a luminaire will produce.

TIP MAINTENANCE

However luminaires are concealed, the designer must ensure that it is possible to access the equipment for future maintenance. A design solution is successful only if it can be maintained to preserve the lit effect that the designer intended.

Below
A lot can be achieved with the simplest luminaires. In this example from a gallery, concealed lighting is mounted within a linear display band. The structure is designed in such a way that a single run of fluorescent battens backlights transparency illustrations in the display band, washes light onto vertical banners behind the band and also illuminates a leaflet shelf below each transparency. This illuminated feature also provides a good deal of the ambient light in the exhibition space.

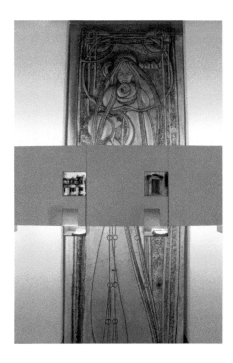

GENERIC LUMINAIRE TYPES

While it may be possible to categorize all luminaires as either dispersive or directional, there are many useful subcategories. There are thousands of lighting manufacturers worldwide, each of whom may have hundreds or thousands of products. At some point in the design process, it is necessary to decide exactly which products will be used for a project, but at the early stages it is much more helpful to set aside specifics and focus on general principles. At concept and scheme design stage, designers will often work with generic luminaire types rather than any specific product. This allows the design to evolve, with the final product selected to fit the completed design proposal rather than the other way round. Any project designed around a particular product is unlikely to be as successful as one where the product is selected to match the particular requirements of the project.

There is no real limit to the number of categories of luminaire, but the following generic list is a useful start.

Incandescent lamp A luminaire can be as basic as a lamp in a lamp holder suspended from a ceiling with rods or wires. In this illustration, the luminaire does not affect the spread of light from the lamp. A bare lamp such as a domestic incandescent produces a fairly equal distribution of light in all directions.

Fluorescent batten A linear fluorescent lamp also has a 360-degree distribution of light. Most of the light is produced at right angles to the tube, with less light directed parallel to the length of the tube. The back box containing the control gear blocks some of the light coming from the back of the lamp, but modern fluorescent gearboxes are slim enough to occlude only a little light.

Compact fluorescent A compact fluorescent lamp is basically a bent and folded linear fluorescent. Domestic compact fluorescent lamps are designed as retrofit replacements for incandescent lamps, and come as a complete package with the control gear housed in the large lamp-holder end of the lamp. This shape means most compact fluorescent lamps do not produce light in all directions as an incandescent lamp does. With little light getting past the control gear housing, their use as replacements in some small domestic table lamps can produce a very unsatisfactory spread of light, which possibly significantly reduces the light output ratio of the luminaire. To be truly efficient, a luminaire needs to be designed around the particular light source used.

Dispersive pendant A simple frosted or opal glass globe luminaire produces a very soft light that is fairly equally spread in all directions. This kind of luminaire can help to disguise the lack of upward light from a suspended, compact fluorescent lamp. With this kind of dispersive luminaire, how brightly a surface is illuminated depends on how far away the surface is from the light source and whether it is facing towards the luminaire.

Downlight pendant The light source used for the dispersive pendant can be fitted into a simple metal shade that redirects the light in one direction, giving control over which surfaces receive most light.

Uplight pendant Suspending the kind of reflector used for the downlight pendant the other way round creates an uplight, which illuminates the soffit to produce a very soft, indirect quality of light.

Floodlights and spotlights A directional luminaire can use any combination of simple shades, polished reflectors or lenses to control the light, and the available range of beam spreads is almost infinite; some luminaires even have an adjustable beam spread. In basic terms, it is enough to describe directional luminaires as wide-beam (also known as floodlights) or narrow-beam (spotlights). The terms 'floodlight' and 'spotlight' are generally applied to discrete, surface-mounted luminaires. A floodlight may be used to evenly illuminate a large area; the narrower spread of light from a spotlight allows small areas and objects to be picked out from their surroundings. Although there is no definition of how wide a spotlight beam has to be before it becomes a floodlight, in normal usage anything above 40 degrees would be too wide to highlight small areas effectively. One definition of beam spread would describe a narrow-beam luminaire as being less than 20 degrees and a medium beam between 20 and 40 degrees. Anything above 40 degrees would be described as a wide beam.

Downlights One of the most common uses of directional luminaires in architectural situations is as downlights recessed into ceiling surfaces. Properly known as ceiling-recessed downlights, this is usually shortened to just downlights. Endless options exist for different light sources, luminaire sizes, shapes and light distributions. The terms 'spotlight' and 'floodlight' are not generally used for recessed luminaires; rather, they tend to be described as medium-, wide- or narrow-beam (or some version of this).

Uplights As with downlights and downlight pendants, uplights can be used in different locations for specific purposes. Floor-standing ones can uplight a soffit where suspended luminaires are not suitable (perhaps because ceiling height is too low). Wall-mounted uplights allow soffits to be illuminated without cluttering the ceiling with pendants. Ground-recessed (or inground) uplights can be used with a diffusing glass as a low-brightness marker or can be used with precision reflectors to illuminate columns or walls from the ground up. Given our natural tendency to look down slightly as we walk, it is good practice to ensure that inground uplights are not in locations where people are likely to walk over them, as they can easily dazzle people.

Reflector shape Floodlight reflectors are usually designed to produce a symmetrical spread of light, but special reflector shapes can produce different spreads of light. Asymmetrical floodlights direct more light to one side than the other. This can be useful where a design calls for wall-mounted uplights to evenly illuminate a soffit from the edges of a room. Asymmetrical reflectors can also be used in ground-recessed uplights to help to evenly illuminate vertical surfaces.

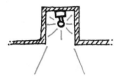

Concealed ceiling coves A fluorescent batten concealed in a ceiling cove can produce a very soft, indirect light that can help to make a low space feel much higher.

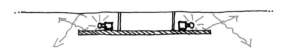

Ceiling slots A concealed fluorescent batten mounted in a ceiling slot uses the architecture as a luminaire to produce controlled and directional light.

Ceiling planes Concealed fluorescent battens mounted above a suspended soffit can create a visual separation between the ceiling planes and make the lowered soffit appear to float below the main ceiling plane. Turn this whole arrangement through 90 degrees and the backlight will make vertical panels float off the wall surface behind.

Visualizing patterns of light

If you imagine you had a perfect lamp that produced an equal amount of light in all directions, the spread of light would be spherical. If you cut a section through the middle of the sphere of light, you would see a circle with the light source at its centre. However, this is theoretical, and real lamps and luminaires do not produce a perfectly even spread of light – in fact, most luminaires are designed to produce something other than a spherical spread of light. Graphical representations can be used to show the pattern of light a luminaire produces.

A fluorescent tube is as close as you may normally get to a lamp that produces light equally in all directions. The proviso is that because it is a linear lamp the spread of light is cylindrical rather than spherical. When viewed end-on, a fluorescent tube by itself produces an even distribution of light over a full 360°. However, a fluorescent lamp is normally used as part of a batten luminaire, and this affects the spread of light from the lamp. Obviously, no light can pass through the gearbox, which causes a shadow, but some of the blocked light will be reflected back, resulting in additional light in certain directions – the spherical distribution of light has been altered significantly. This information can be described with a polar intensity diagram, which represents a section slice through the luminaire, with the spread of light shown as a curved line.

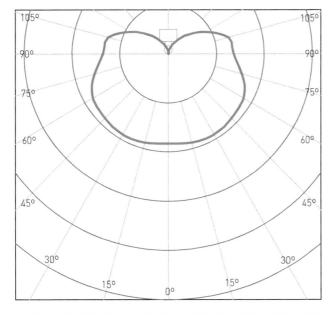

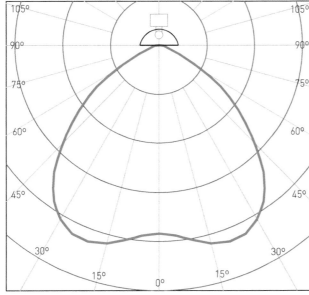

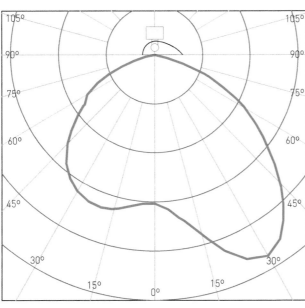

Top left

The polar intensity diagram is produced by taking lighting measurements all the way around the luminaire and drawing a curve – the red lines in these diagrams describe the light intensity on a plane through the centre of the luminaire. The influence of the luminaire on the shape of the blue intensity curve is clear to see. The top of the curve is flattened because the gearbox is interrupting the light going upwards from the lamp, and some of that light is reflected downwards, giving a slight bulge at around 30° from the vertical. This illustration and the two that follow include drawings of luminaires to make understanding the diagram easier. However, in practice the luminaire is not usually shown in a polar intensity diagram.

Centre left

In this example, the red line represents the polar intensity curve for the fluorescent batten after it has been fitted with a polished reflector. The reflector stops all light from escaping upwards and redirects it downwards, creating a real direction to the distribution of light. This diagram can also help you to visualize other features of the luminaire. You will see that the intensity curve does not extend above 60° from the vertical. This is because the reflector is preventing any light escaping at a higher angle. If you positioned the luminaire near a vertical surface, no direct light would hit the surface above this 60° line. This could result in a very visible shadow line.

Bottom left

In the previous two examples, the spread of light has been symmetrical – the same on either side of the vertical. Here, the reflector shape has been designed to produce an asymmetrical distribution of light. This polar intensity curve shows a clear peak on the right-hand side. You will also see that the luminaire produces light up to about 75° from the vertical, which means there would be a much smaller area of shadow if it were placed near a vertical surface. This kind of asymmetrical reflector is often used to provide an even illumination for vertical surfaces.

Top right

This illuminance cone diagram for a 50 W low-voltage spotlight records a minimal amount of data. The lamp or luminaire is assumed to be positioned at the top centre of the chart, facing directly downwards. All measurements are taken on a horizontal plane perpendicular to the lamp. The numbers on the left show the distance from the lamp at which the measurements were taken. The right-hand figures show the lux level, at those distances. For a spotlight, these numbers will be the peak, or maximum, lux level. With this chart, there is no way of knowing how even the lux levels are across the beam, or whether the peak is in the centre of the beam. The beam angle of the lamp is described by the manufacturer as being 40°. However, that may be an approximation, so the centre column of numbers shows the actual beam diameter at different distances. It is important to realize that these measurements do not refer to the total spread of the light; the light does not stop beyond the 40° line. The beam angle quoted for the lamp actually relates to the angle at which the light level will be 50% of the peak – this is referred to as the half peak beam angle.

Bottom right

The half peak beam angle used to describe a spotlight is best understood with a polar diagram. In this example, increasing distance from the chart origin (the junction of the 0° and 90° lines) relates to increasing intensity. For this luminaire, the peak output is not perpendicular to the spotlight, it is slightly to the side at around 20° from the vertical. For this luminaire, we would say the half peak beam angle was 102° – the angle at which the output is half the maximum output. In the case of this luminaire, the light falls off very quickly above the half peak angle. Other luminaires may have very different characteristics.

Visualizing spotlight data

Full polar diagrams are rarely made for spotlight luminaires and spotlamps. This type of luminaire is considered to produce a conical beam of light, and this is described in a simplified diagram – an illuminance cone diagram. This uses much less data than the polar diagram, but is designed to give a reasonable understanding of the lit effect.

50 W, 40° low-voltage dichroic lamp

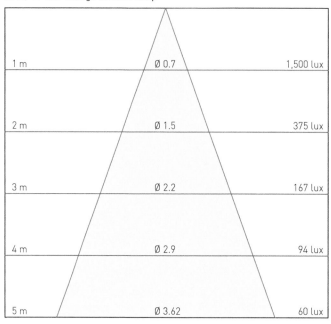

1 m	Ø 0.7	1,500 lux
2 m	Ø 1.5	375 lux
3 m	Ø 2.2	167 lux
4 m	Ø 2.9	94 lux
5 m	Ø 3.62	60 lux

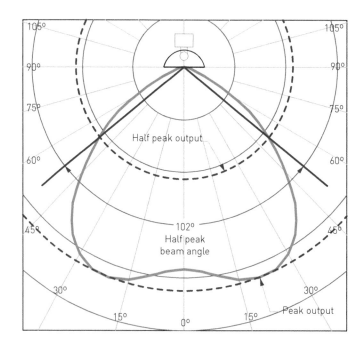

Isolux diagrams

Isolux diagrams can be used to display the light
distribution of a luminaire, but they are most commonly
used to show the pattern of light produced by many
luminaires in a lighting design. The diagram below shows
the light landing on a single surface. Because an isolux
diagram is just an illustration of the light arriving at the
surface – the illuminance – it can tell us little about how
bright a surface will actually appear to a viewer – the
luminance. That is a complex question that relies heavily
on the colour, texture and reflectivity of the surface being
illuminated.

Left
An isolux diagram is the lighting
equivalent of a contour map.
Where a contour map shows
lines that link areas of equal
height, an isolux diagram shows
lines of equal illuminance. This
diagram maps the lux levels
measured at ground level for a
70 W metal halide floodlight
mounted 3 m above the ground
level. The luminaire is located at
0,0 on the chart (indicated by the
X) and is mounted so that it faces
the measuring plane. The diagram
helps us understand the spread
of light from the asymmetrical
floodlight.

70 W metal halide asymmetric floodlight mounted at 3 m

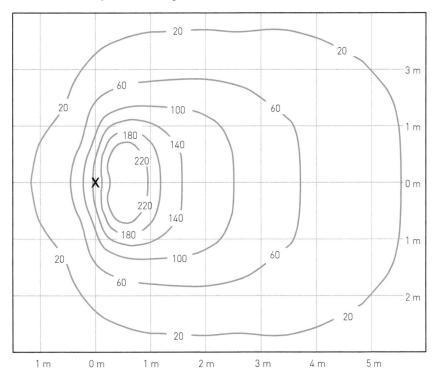

Lighting control systems

The control of lighting should be at the heart of any design proposal. At the very least, it needs to be capable of being switched on and off by the end users. But there are many reasons to consider a more elaborate method of controlling lighting.

Even in very small spaces, it is likely that not all the lighting will need to be on at all times. It may be switched on or off in response to changes in external lighting conditions; changes in the user's activity may require more or less light; lighting may be changed to create different atmospheres; when users leave the room it may be switched off automatically to save energy; it may be changed dynamically to create visual interest. All these possible scenarios suggest that the designer needs to consider carefully how lighting will be controlled so as to allow for the kind of interaction required.

At the simplest level, the designer should consider which luminaires should be controlled together – that is, which ones will always switch on and off at the same time – and which need to be controlled independently.

Opposite and left
Even relatively modest hotel rooms contain many options in terms of the control of lighting. This one in Bern, Switzerland, allows guests to dim the lighting in order to set the ambience they require. The lighting is also separately circuited, allowing some luminaires to be switched off while others are kept on. The luminaires here account for four circuits of control; the room also contains another floor-standing lamp, an entrance luminaire and a bathroom light. While this is much more control than one would typically expect in such a small area, the multiuse nature of the space means that the designers wanted to give the users the maximum flexibility to select the lighting that suits them best. This sequence of images clearly demonstrates the layers of lighting that experienced designers use to create a lit scene. As in this example, layers of light may be controlled independently or the designer may simply use changes of intensity, colour or direction to create a visual richness.

Mains voltage dimming

The intricate detail of how dimmers work is a very technical subject and does not really need to concern us. Nonetheless, it is useful to know why all dimmers may not be equal.

The mains electricity used in any grid-connected building is supplied by the electricity company in the form of alternating current (AC). This fluctuates very quickly, at around 50–60 times every second, between positive and negative polarity. When a tungsten lamp is connected to a mains supply it is actually being fed a voltage that rises from zero to full power and falls back again. This happens so fast that the voltage is rising again before the lamp filament has a chance to cool down and reduce its light output – there is therefore no visible flickering and the light stays on at full brightness. Low-voltage tungsten lighting operates in a similar fashion to its mains voltage counterpart, but it relies on a transformer to reduce the mains voltage to the low voltage appropriate for the lamp. Modern transformers are highly sophisticated electronic devices that are designed to provide the ideal electrical supply for a specific lamp. High-quality transformers often contain other circuitry that can help to maintain good lamp life by filtering out electrical anomalies that could be damaging.

Rather than the light source always being at full brightness, you may want to have the option of sometimes reducing the light level. Dimmers allow you to do this, but they introduce another electronic device into the chain and there can often be incompatibilities between dimmers and transformers. This can result in poor operation or even the failure of one of the devices.

Leaving aside the obvious issues of ensuring that equipment and wiring are not overloaded, there can be more esoteric problems. Not all transformers are dimmable, so it is important to check. It is also important to realize that not all dimmable transformers can be dimmed with all types of dimmer, and it is worth trying to understand why this may be the case.

When you connect a tungsten light source to a mains voltage power supply you are connecting it to an alternating current (AC), as previously described. The cycle of rising and falling voltages follows a smooth sine wave. A dimmer changes this pattern to reduce the amount of electricity flowing to the lamp. Most dimmers are crude devices that chop a slice out of the cycle so that the lamp is effectively switched off for a small period of time. Two forms of simple dimmer operate in this fashion. The leading edge dimmer switches off the power as the voltage is about to increase. Where it switches on again in the cycle determines the extent to which the light is reduced. The main advantage of this kind of dimmer is that it is relatively easy and cheap to make. The problem is that it

Right and opposite
The sine wave of an AC power supply is chopped by a traditional dimmer to reduce the light output of dimmable luminaires. Leading edge dimming creates a sudden jump as the voltage rises. Trailing edge dimming is gentler on electronic devices and is likely to be compatible with more kinds of transformer. Sine wave dimming takes a different approach to reducing the power to the lamp. It is compatible with many more types of lamp and control gear, but it is much more expensive.

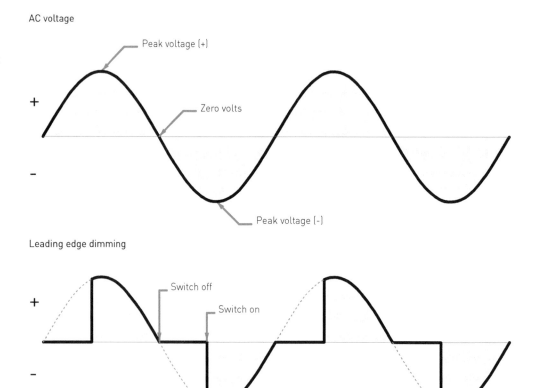

AC voltage

Peak voltage (+)

+

Zero volts

–

Peak voltage (-)

Leading edge dimming

+

Switch off

Switch on

–

produces a very abrupt change from zero voltage to full voltage, and it is difficult for electronic transformers to deal with this. Trailing edge dimmers also chop the sine wave, but they switch off as the voltage is falling. The result is a gradual increase in voltage with an abrupt drop to zero. This is much kinder on transformer electronics, and the components of the transformer are less expensive than those for a leading edge dimmer, but the dimmer itself requires more expensive electronics.

Always check the specification of electronic transformers to ensure they are dimmable and determine whether they need trailing edge dimming. Generally speaking, a leading edge dimmer only dims a leading edge dimmable transformer successfully. A trailing edge dimmer normally dims both leading and trailing edge dimmable transformers.

A sine wave dimmer works with leading or trailing edge transformers and may even dim metal halide lamps. It is a much more sophisticated device that can maintain the smooth waveform of the AC sine wave but reduces the overall amplitude to decrease light levels. Sine wave dimmers are relatively rare as they are expensive and metal halide dimming is not always 100 per cent reliable.

Dimmable versions of LED light sources are often available, but the technology is varied and differs from dimming incandescents, so check their compatibility with dimming systems.

TIP COMPATIBILITY

No matter what kind of light source you want to dim, compatibility should be the first concern. Not all luminaires are dimmable; even luminaires with notionally dimmable light sources, such as low-voltage tungsten halogen, may not have dimmable transformers. Even having a dimmable light source and a 'dimmable' transformer/ballast/ driver does not ensure success unless you know that the dimmer is fully compatible with that kind of device. It is always wise to confirm compatibility with the manufacturers of the dimming equipment.

Trailing edge dimming

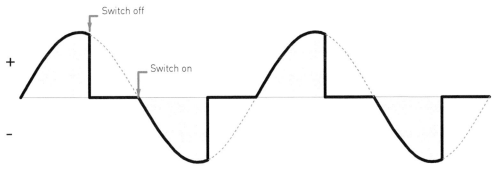

Sine wave dimming

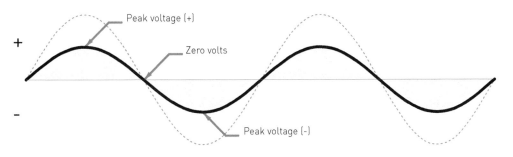

Electronic dimming

Traditional mains dimming systems rely on discrete dimming devices to alter the voltage supplied to the luminaire, but this is not the only way of controlling lighting. Many systems combine the dimming control with the electronics of the transformers or control gear that operate the lamp. This means the dimming is tuned specifically to the lamp type being used, and control can be extended to individual lamps instead of groups of all the luminaires on one electrical circuit.

Electronic dimming removes the need for a dedicated dimmer unit, but it does require a control signal between the operating device (wall switch, motion detector, fader or daylight sensor) and the control gear. Several protocols exist for the communication between controller and luminaire. Some of the most common light-specific methods include the analogue 0–10 volt control, where a change in a low-voltage control signal results in a proportional change in the output of the lamp. Analogue control requires one set of wires for each control channel. Digital control allows many channels of control to be sent down one cable.

Digital control systems for lighting include DALI, DMX and DSI. These systems are not compatible with each other and each has its own limitations. Great care has to be taken to select the most appropriate kind of control. As a simple example, in a DALI system the lighting scenes are usually stored in each DALI device (for example, a transformer or fluorescent control gear). This allows each device to work with a degree of autonomy if required; each luminaire can be controlled by an onboard daylight or presence sensor. The DALI protocol is relatively slow and is best suited to locations where lighting changes are fairly limited and repeatable, such as office spaces and general public spaces.

On the other hand, some situations require very fast and dynamic control of large numbers of luminaires with multiple functions such as colour change, movement, dimming and beam control – the kind of equipment typically used in entertainment settings. DMX is the preferred protocol in this situation. as it is capable of operating many more channels than DALI and at a much faster rate, allowing for quick lighting changes to be effected. DMX systems tend to have all the intelligence at the controller end, with each device reliant on the instructions from the remotely located controller. Luminaires that involve colour change or movement, or are used in entertainment settings, are likely to be DMX-controlled, whereas DALI luminaires tend to predominate in general architectural spaces such as offices.

While it is possible to find devices that allow one device protocol to be controlled by another, the systems tend to be designed around very different functions and it should not be assumed that the same results can be achieved. A typical DALI dimmable fluorescent will continue to respond at a very sedate pace even if it is interfaced to a DMX controller – it is designed to work that way. Control system integration is quite a specialist task and, for this reason, many systems are not simply specified, but are custom-configured by the manufacturer to a plan produced by the lighting designer. This means the designer needs to be able to identify explicitly the kind of control and user interaction that is required for each part of his or her lighting installation.

TIP DIGITAL CONTROL SYSTEMS

DSI and DALI: Digital Signal Interface (DSI) is a protocol for sending digital dimming control signals to luminaire control gear. DSI is a simple system that allows dimming over a range of 0–255 steps, but requires one wire for each control channel. Therefore, multiple dimming channels require multiple control wires, which can complicate large installations. DSI is also a proprietary standard created by ballast manufacturer Tridonic and owned by parent company Zumtobel. DSI has largely been replaced by the Digital Addressable Lighting Interface (DALI) protocol. DALI is an open standard and is used by many lighting manufacturers (including Zumtobel). Unlike DSI, DALI can independently control up to 64 devices on one pair of control wires. Each device is given an address number from 0 to 63 and then responds only to data sent to its unique address or to data broadcast for all devices. Systems using multiple groups of 64 devices can create larger installations. In addition to output devices such as dimmable control gear and transformers, it is possible to use DSI and DALI to interface input devices such as switches, motion sensors, daylight sensors and remote control receivers.

Left

Natural light is a constantly changing mosaic of colour and texture. There is no reason why lighting for the built environment should be any different. With the aid of a programmable lighting control system, users can select different lighting scenes. Scenes can also be recalled automatically at different times of day or in response to people movement, external weather conditions or the state of the stock market. The lobby of this high-end workspace has no natural light, but displays a constantly shifting pattern of light and colour to stimulate the employees and the visitors. These three images show just a selection of the many different looks that the system cycles through. A dappled light falls over the seating and the walls are enlivened with projections. These three scenes could allude to the quality of light at different times of day: cool blue morning, bright daytime and golden sunset. The coloured vertical surface in the distance is the outside wall of a small meeting space where the whole ambience of the room can be altered by changing the colour of the walls. The selection of colour allows the room to be relaxing, vibrant, contemplative or energizing depending on the requirements of the users.

PART II PROCESS AND PRACTICE

5. Lighting principles

Despite being the most critical part of the design process, the principles of lighting are often not well defined. A lighting design is most robust when it is built on the foundation of a strong conceptual approach. Well-defined and coherent lighting principles also allow the lighting design to evolve naturally as the architecture, brief and budget are revised throughout the design and construction process.

Visual hierarchy

During the day, it is easy to think that the natural world has one principal light source in the shape of the sun. However, our surroundings are always illuminated by a combination of direct light from the sun and sky and light that comes from a multitude of directions and is reflected by clouds, plants, ground, snow, water and rocks. Each light source or source of reflected light has its own qualities of intensity, direction, colour and diffusion. Each source and reflection adds something, however small, to our visual environment. Even in the harshest glare of unfiltered equatorial sunlight, the naturally lit scene is defined not by a single source and single direction

Left
The illumination of the Great Hall at Stirling Castle, Scotland, is built with layers of light to create the correct visual balance.

Opposite
Much of the lighting in the Great Hall is mounted at the wall head with 70 W metal halide uplights to reveal the hammer-beam oak roof (A). To prevent glare for visitors looking up from ground level, the ambient light is bounced off the limewashed white walls using 70 W metal halide spotlights (B), with 150 W metal halide floodlights providing a wash down to around head height on the wall hangings (C). Narrow-beam tungsten halogen spotlights pick out the heraldic crest (D) and recessed fibre-optic downlights illuminate the fireplace recesses (E). At night, low-voltage tungsten halogen spotlights uplight the reveals of the bay windows to replace the daylight (F). All these elements are controlled independently so each layer can be turned off as required. In addition, moving mirror-effect projectors provide direct light to the floor area for special evening functions, such as concerts or dinners (G). A ground-level control panel allows these projectors to be rotated to focus on the stage area or main floor. If required, the projectors can be programmed to provide coloured light. Lighting by Speirs and Major Associates.

of light, but by multiple directions, intensities and colour qualities of direct and reflected light. It is these combinations that give rise to the richness of our visual experience. To create interior environments with the same naturalistic feel, we should embrace the notion of using multiple layers of light that combine to produce a complete scene.

Light can be a powerful medium to establish the kind of visual hierarchy that we seek in interior spaces. The simple choice of whether to illuminate a surface or object directly affects the way it is perceived by the viewer. We can choose to conceal less attractive areas by concentrating light where we want people to look; we can make an area advance or retreat visually with the subtle use of colour; intensity and direction of light can also provide subtle

signals about what is most visually important in the scene in front of us.

To be able to use the visual hierarchy of light successfully, we need to get into the minds of the users of different kinds of space. An environment where people are agitated and need to find their bearings quickly, such as the entrance to a hospital emergency wing, requires a very different visual hierarchy to an environment where people wish to linger and spend lots of time, such as a museum or gallery. In either case, it is imagining or visualizing the scene from both the users' point of view and their mindset that makes it possible to create the most appropriate lighting solution.

Understanding qualities of natural light

If we want a space to have a legible and familiar feel, we can work with the qualities of natural light. By endeavouring to replicate or reinforce the direction, colour, intensity and variation of natural light, we can fashion an environment that has the familiar quality of the exterior world. Given our species' physiological and psychological adaption and predisposition to natural light over millennia of evolution, this approach should provide an easily understandable lit environment.

Conversely, it is easy to produce surprising and discordant environments by working against the patterns of light and colour that we may expect to see in the outside world. This can be used to attract people's attention, or to subtly discourage them from entering a space by lighting it in an uninviting manner.

Studies of good and bad examples of existing lighting installations can often be informed by applying a naturalistic view to them. Does the bad example exhibit lighting qualities that would not be found in natural light, or that signify the kind of natural environment that has a negative effect on people – is the quality of light reminiscent of an overcast day before a heavy rainstorm? Does the good lighting example have clear parallels with the kind of natural light we enjoy; are important features strongly illuminated as if they were caught in a shaft of sunlight?

Whether or not we choose to work with them, as designers we should be aware of the qualities that define natural light.

Left A low-light space such as this museum tends to feel gloomy. This can be counteracted by introducing some sense of natural light. In this example, the lighting designers created an artificial sky vault over the display cases, using blue cold cathode luminaires concealed in a trough. This inverted the usual experience of a dark soffit in this kind of low-light gallery, making the space seem much brighter than it actually is.

Understanding layers of light

A landscape seen on a bright sunny day may look as though it is illuminated solely by the sun. However, the sky is a major contributor of additional light. When it is clear blue it can supply a large amount of indirect sunlight at ground level. Consider the sky as a dome that sails high overhead and stretches down to the horizon in every direction. The direct light we receive from this sky dome comes from all directions above the horizon line. For this reason, it is not directional and therefore does not create strong shadows – it produces a diffuse quality of light.

Sunlight reflects off clouds in the different levels of the atmosphere and off solid surfaces at ground level. Areas that are shaded from direct sunlight or sky light can still receive natural light that has been reflected from the ground, foliage, water, snow and buildings. The reflected light often picks up the colour of the reflecting surface, and smooth shiny surfaces can focus it to create patches of

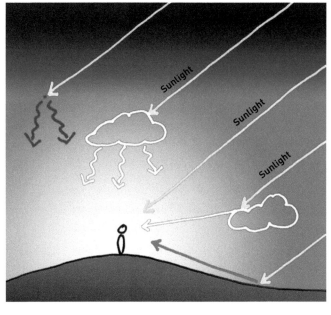

Left

Where controlled daylight is allowed into an interior space, replicating the direction it comes from allows artificial lighting to gradually take over as the daylight fades. In this example, the lighting designers mounted wall-wash spotlights on a lighting track attached to the roof-light glazing bars. These luminaires can be switched off when there is sufficient daylight to illuminate the space, and can be gradually faded in to supplement daylight on dull days or in the evening.

Above

Direct sunlight is only one component of natural light. Small particles in the upper atmosphere cause Rayleigh scattering of sunlight. The blue part of the spectrum is scattered most strongly, hence the blue of the sky. Direct sunlight is reflected by clouds, with much of it being reflected away from the surface of the earth. Clouds also transmit sunlight, which is diffused and softened by its passage through the water and ice they contain. On heavily overcast days, this diffusion can produce an almost directionless quality to light at ground level, with almost no discernible shadows. Some sunlight is reflected by surfaces at ground level. Sunlight is the most directional of all the components of natural light and produces the strongest and best-defined shadows.

higher intensity, such as the moving pattern of undulating light reflected from rippling water.

Light in the natural world is all about the layering of light from multiple directions: strong directional light mingling with softer diffuse light, white light with subtle tints picked up from the sky and reflecting surfaces. This mixture changes constantly, providing a new pattern of light and shade every time we look. By comparison, most artificially lit working environments have uniform lighting; the light tends to come from only one direction and any reflected light is accidental and dependent on the furniture and fittings in the space below the lights. Even though pattern, texture and shadow provide a massive amount of visual richness in the natural world, they tend to be deliberately excluded from most artificially lit interiors. It is no wonder that, with the light and wonder of the natural world designed out of them, many workplaces feel so uninspiring, cold and clinical.

Right
This internal staircase in the Louvre museum in Paris receives no direct natural light, but the indirect uplight reflected from the vaulted soffit replicates the typical conditions of a daylit sky.

Change and variation

In Part 1 we discussed the changing nature of light over 24-hour and yearly cycles. Add to this the ever-changing vagaries and beauty created by weather systems and we have something remarkable. Even if we never move from our vantage point and never alter our direction of view, the light around us is still constantly changing. This continual and restless change defines light in the natural world. A designer should never underestimate the richness of experience this adds to the visual world.

When designing the lighting for built environments, we need to remember that change and variation in light are expected in a natural environment. We may not always have to involve sophisticated control systems to achieve suitable changes in artificial worlds. In most types of building these may be unnecessary because, within them, people move from one space to another. Creating areas with subtly differing qualities of light adds a visual richness to the experience of being within a space. Small and deliberate changes in light colour, colour temperature, intensity, direction and focus in different parts of the space are easy to implement and can transform an otherwise drab experience. To achieve the best possible design outcome, the designer should use light and colour to carefully plan the visual experience for the user, rather than simply using light to illuminate 'task areas'.

Left
A typical office space is designed to be flexible in its layout. This tends to result in lighting installations that aim for high degrees of uniformity. The typical installation has very little contrast or variation of direction, colour or changes in illumination levels over the course of a day. A desk placed in the centre of the space receives the same quantity and quality of light whether it is day or night. This situation is not always completely in the control of the designer, as many lighting standards and codes of practice for this kind of environment insist on high levels of uniformity.

Creating drama through lighting

For something to be dramatic, it must eschew the ordinary, the commonplace and the predictable. It should be striking, unusual and even completely unexpected. By this definition, what we tend to experience on a daily basis is not dramatic. The thrill is in the perfect combination of atmospheric conditions that presents us with a dazzling rainbow arcing across the sky; it is a once-yearly fleeting angle of sunlight that pushes between mountain tops to isolate the tip of a snowy peak in an amber spotlight.

Sunlight does not care what it illuminates, but as designers we can be more discriminating. We can make conscious decisions about what should be visually important and what should recede into the background, and design the lighting accordingly. To make an object or surface stand out does not necessitate using very bright light sources – all that is needed is a good control of contrast. Creating a hierarchy of visual importance and working with layers of light should ensure that the significant features of a space are not lost among uniformly illuminated surroundings.

Dramatic lighting can come from the choice of lighting directions, colour combinations, the pattern of light and shade or the changing nature of any of these elements. But drama requires novelty, so the more an effect is used the more commonplace it becomes. Spectacular lighting demands innovation and careful choreography to maintain the element of surprise.

Far left
A shaft of sunlight entering through high-level clerestory glazing catches the sculpture and isolates it from its surroundings.

Left
The unnatural direction of the strong uplight and the blood-red ambient light enhance the drama of this life-size figure in a tableau at a visitor centre.

Above
Despite the strong visual clues of overlapping layers of hills and the aerial perspective that fades and dulls the distant mountain, a patch of intense sunlight can make part of the landscape seem to leap forward. The clarity and intensity of light in the sunlit patch suggest it must be closer to the viewer than it really is. The fact that it is surrounded by relatively dark surfaces further elevates the visual importance of this part of the scene.

Right
Theatrical lighting techniques are often employed in architectural situations to enhance the sense of being somewhere else. The lighting designer used coloured light, projections of clouds and light shining on a scenic palm to create the feeling of a desert island for a storytelling corner in an exhibition.

Changing and controlling light

Natural light is rarely static, so it is perhaps strange that much interior lighting only has two states: on or off. There are many reasons for lighting to change or be controlled. In the current climate, reducing electrical loads and therefore running costs is one of the most important. If a space is adequately illuminated at certain times by daylight, it would be sensible to ensure that artificial lighting is switched off. Unfortunately, studies have shown that once lights are switched on in a typical working environment, users rarely switch them off until they leave at the end of the day. A lighting control system with photocells that track light levels, either externally or inside a room, can automate the process of turning lights off when they are not required. Simple motion detectors can be integrated into luminaires or control systems to ensure lights are switched off when rooms are vacated.

Right
In its normal temple surroundings, this statue of the Hindu deity Shiva would typically be illuminated by the light of sputtering oil lamps. This would cast multiple shadows of the dancing figure, which would jump around as the light flickered. For this display, the designer designed two custom luminaires that were recessed in the soffit in front of the statue. The luminaires contain a revolving textured glass disc that interrupts and distorts the light from two low-voltage lamps. The result is a gently flickering set of shadows that appear to be animated as if the statue were lit by oil lamps.

Left and above

During the day, this narrow perimeter atrium gives a daylit feel to the internal office spaces through extensive roof glazing and vertical glazing on the external façade. At night, the daylight is replaced by 400 W metal halide spotlights with daylight colour temperature lamps. The luminaires are positioned to bounce light off the white, internal surface of the façade, to increase the luminance of the wall when seen from the internal office spaces.

This page and opposite
Bars and restaurants see much of their custom at night and we tend to think of most of them as being dimly illuminated with a cosy atmosphere. This bar and restaurant is open during the day as well as at night. The designer has created contrasting atmospheres for day and night. The daytime lighting (above) is crisp and white, and blends well with daylight entering the space around the perimeter. At night (left), the lights dim to produce a warm, comforting glow, and some lights are switched off. Red LED uplights integrated into the window sills (right and far right) give an atmospheric red glow to the translucent curtains. This creates a strong brand image when seen from the street.

Changes in lighting can also be enacted by timers that select from a preset series of lighting effects. For a hotel lobby or restaurant, these may include a number of different looks that are selected at different times of the day to suit the prevailing conditions for breakfast, mid-morning, lunch, afternoon, evening meal, late evening and overnight. The changes between these different states should take place over a period of at least several minutes so as to appear seamless to customers.

While control systems allow sophisticated automated control of lighting, it is worth remembering that, especially in working environments, people need to feel that they can influence their surroundings. A lack of control is an often-cited feature of poor working environments, and something as simple as allowing employees to have their own desk lights can greatly improve their satisfaction. Of course, many of the desk lights will not be switched off at night, so it is still a good idea to have overall master control of all the lighting.

Change and control of lighting can also be employed to add dynamism to interior spaces. Where changes happen relatively quickly, they are very noticeable and can be used to attract attention or add a level of activity and excitement. As a form of dramatic lighting, successful dynamic designs use change sparingly and form areas of relative calm to provide contrast with any movement or colour change.

A The footprints and ripples of sand in this image are nothing more than changes in light and shade. The patterns have been revealed by low-angle sunlight; they could be lost under a shadowless overcast sky.

B Without the grazing light, the three-dimensional quality of the carving could be lost on the casual viewer. The angle at which light strikes a surface and the contrast with any ambient light determines the extent to which the texture or form is enhanced.

C With ground-level low-voltage uplights deliberately mounted very close to the rough stone wall, its texture is enhanced.

D Even where surfaces have no texture, pattern can be introduced with light. This traditional Arabic lantern is an interesting object when illuminated by the internal glow of a clear tungsten lamp. But the real magic is created when a thousand pinpricks of light are scattered over the surrounding walls. The pattern of light filtered through a perforated material is very evocative. Yet, without adjacent surfaces, it would remain invisible.

Surfaces and texture

Light is about surface. Without a surface to capture and reflect the light, we will see nothing. Visualizing yourself in a space and 'seeing' which surfaces are most important and prominent will help you to decide where the lighting should be positioned.

Surface itself is about texture. Materials can be smooth, rough, patterned, reflective or matt. The combination of textural qualities should guide your choice of light source and locations to ensure that you can enhance or conceal the texture, or so that you can avoid glare from reflective surfaces but still create enough sparkle to prevent them becoming dull and lifeless.

Below and right

It is clear from looking at the luminaire locations in the section drawing of part of the Pier Shops at Caesars, Atlantic City, NJ, that Focus Lighting has designed a project that is all about surfaces. Relatively little light is directed towards the ground, as this would not help the space feel well lit if there were no vertical illumination. The photograph shows how textural surfaces are enhanced by the lighting; some textural elements are entirely created by it. The water effect on the soffit panels is produced with theatrical projection equipment that creates a constantly moving effect of light reflected from moving water.

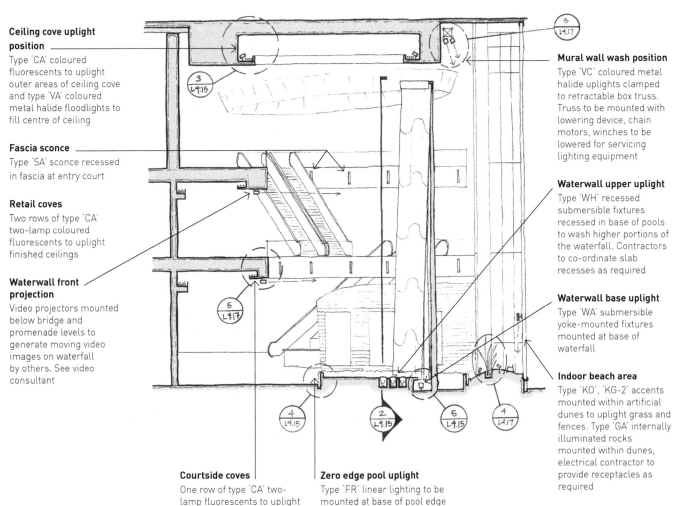

Ceiling cove uplight position

Type 'CA' coloured fluorescents to uplight outer areas of ceiling cove and type 'VA' coloured metal halide floodlights to fill centre of ceiling

Fascia sconce

Type 'SA' sconce recessed in fascia at entry court

Retail coves

Two rows of type 'CA' two-lamp coloured fluorescents to uplight finished ceilings

Waterwall front projection

Video projectors mounted below bridge and promenade levels to generate moving video images on waterfall by others. See video consultant

Courtside coves

One row of type 'CA' two-lamp fluorescents to uplight finished ceiling

Zero edge pool uplight

Type 'FR' linear lighting to be mounted at base of pool edge to uplight pool side walls. Type 'LFR' power supplies as needed mounted within accessible locations

Mural wall wash position

Type 'VC' coloured metal halide uplights clamped to retractable box truss. Truss to be mounted with lowering device, chain motors, winches to be lowered for servicing lighting equipment

Waterwall upper uplight

Type 'WH' recessed submersible fixtures recessed in base of pools to wash higher portions of the waterfall. Contractors to co-ordinate slab recesses as required

Waterwall base uplight

Type 'WA' submersible yoke-mounted fixtures mounted at base of waterfall

Indoor beach area

Type 'KO', 'KG-2' accents mounted within artificial dunes to uplight grass and fences. Type 'GA' internally illuminated rocks mounted within dunes, electrical contractor to provide receptacles as required

6. Lighting for people

Ultimately, architectural lighting is all about people, but often their needs seem to be secondary to what is inexpensive or easy to achieve. However, lighting that is properly designed with users in mind should be cost-effective. So, what do people really need when it comes to lighting?

How much light is enough?

Every country has lighting codes and standards that are intended to give guidance about how much light should be used to create well-lit spaces. Standards are often broken down to provide recommendations based on the activity patterns of different kinds of space, from entrance lobbies, corridors, offices and gymnasia through to the platforms of underground stations. These standards are considered to be best practice and are sometimes minimum legal requirements for lighting. They are usually based on research into how well a group of test subjects performs a range of tasks in experimental lighting conditions.

A quick look at any set of lighting standards shows recommendations such as 200 lux on the floor of an entrance lobby, 100 lux on the floor of a corridor, 300 lux average at desk height in a classroom (with a uniformity of 80 per cent) or 500 lux for a game of five-a-side football. These variations are related to the difficulty of the visual task and the level of hazard involved, so walking along a corridor is judged to require less light than reading printed documents or playing fast-moving ball games.

Many standards form contractual or legal requirements that the designer has to satisfy, but designing to a standard or code of practice does not guarantee a building that the users see as being well lit. In fact, over-reliance on working to code without actually thinking about how the light will affect the users,

architecture and surfaces has often produced bad lighting. A good designer considers codes and standards to be minimum requirements and certainly not prescriptions for how to design: people simply do not perceive lit environments in the way that they are measured with a lux meter.

The case study of St Machar's Cathedral (see pages 130–9) describes the lighting design process for relighting a religious building to suit the needs of tourists and worshippers. The cathedral's congregation is predominantly over the age of 45, so their eyesight is significantly poorer than that of the average 20-year-old, but the level of light around the pews did not cause them major concern as hymn books could be read acceptably in the existing lighting. Typical guidance would suggest a light level of at least 100 lux or possibly 200 lux for this function. In fact, the measured light levels at the pews varied from a maximum of 40 lux down to 20 lux. The measured light levels were low and suggested a dark space, but, importantly, this was not the perception of the users of the building. The psychological experience was of a space that was naturally lit during the day and, with the existing tungsten lighting, the electric lighting had a very high colour quality that largely replicated the pattern of the natural light. In short, the users did not feel the space to be dark at night.

The perception of brightness can sometimes be far more important than the actual measured light level. Without light on the vertical surfaces (the surfaces we actually tend to look at), it would be possible to create a space that seemed very dark despite having plenty of light at ground level.

Lighting codes and standards can certainly provide some guidance, but to create a well-lit space a good designer does more than simply calculate the light reaching the floor.

Opposite
Interior detail of Peter Zumthor's Bruder Klaus Kapelle, Mechernich, Germany. Despite high levels of natural light on the ground, the darkness of the vertical surfaces makes the space feel very dark. The illuminance of the ground plane is no measure of the apparent lightness of a space.

Lighting for comfort and safety

Emergency lighting is a particular area of lighting design that requires careful examination of the relevant codes and standards to ensure compliance. In an emergency where the power has failed, battery-backed lighting is designed to switch on automatically to ensure there is a suitable level of light to allow safe exit from the building. Like the recommendations for normal lighting, emergency lighting requirements vary depending on the activity. High-risk areas, such as places with fast-moving machinery, require a higher light level than the lobby of an office building. Given the illuminance levels and high uniformity often suggested for normal usage, it is instructive to realize that the most critical lighting situation, an emergency evacuation, may require an office lobby to be illuminated to a minimum of only 0.5 lux. Safety lighting has very different criteria from normal lighting requirements.

Looking beyond emergency lighting situations, comfort and safety may sometimes be seen to be unconnected. Nonetheless, any lighting installation that makes the user feel uncomfortable, perhaps through excessive glare or contrast, is unlikely to engender a feeling of safety. But what kind of light makes us feel safe?

It is not possible to feel comfortable without feeling safe. In a scale of primal needs, for any animal, safety is much more fundamental than comfort, which is a nice extra to be aspired to. This seems to be the general approach taken with much of the lighting in public spaces, which is often designed to cover basic safety and task needs; anything else is an embellishment that may be nice to have but is not essential. However, this is where designers who work from the viewpoint of the end user can effect real change. If we can design lighting that starts with what makes a lit environment special, and we can deliver it in a way that is comfortable for the user, we will have already created a sense of safety, and probably covered many of the task-lighting requirements.

Above left
Emergency lighting in public buildings is powered by batteries or by an independent power supply to ensure that interiors are not plunged into complete darkness in the event of a power failure. Surface-mounted luminaires are a common solution, but the unsightly results are often an indication of a lack of co-ordination between the overall design and the emergency lighting. Where the latter is independent of general lighting, modern LED light sources allow emergency luminaires to be very small and discreet. In this photograph, the solid rhythm created by the patches of light and shade is broken by the ceiling-mounted emergency luminaire next to the first exit sign. This visual disruption is really not necessary.

Above right
Although there are no exit signs visible in this image, the corridor does have emergency lighting. The recessed continuous-channel luminaire for linear fluorescent lamps (on the left side of the corridor) provides the principal lighting for the space. A small number of these lamps are also supplied from an emergency lighting power supply so that they will remain on if there is a power failure. The emergency lighting has been co-ordinated with the general lighting and the result is a seamless integrated solution.

Task lighting

Task lighting forms the basis of most lighting standards. These sometimes suggest lighting direction for different kinds of task, but most standards are focused on the quantity of light needed. As ever, good lighting requires much more than simply complying with the relevant standards. Whatever the activity, we should imagine ourselves in the position of the users so that we can visualize exactly what they require. We need to ensure that the lighting we design does nothing to hinder the task at hand. This could include designing out glare from reflective surfaces or visible light sources; it could be as basic as ensuring that users do not cast shadows on the object they are trying to examine because of badly positioned luminaires. Task lighting is often seen to be the light required for the immediate activity of reading, typing or operating machinery, but a good designer should consider a much wider definition. Someone working at a detailed task does not exist in an isolated bubble, and the designer should view the whole lit environment as contributing to the task light. A high level of light on a book does not help the reader to concentrate if the surrounding space seems dark and dangerous.

Good task lighting creates a good combination of intensity and direction that suits a particular activity, but in many instances allowing some personal control provides the best user experience. A sense of control is always significant in workplace satisfaction surveys, and it is easy to provide this with locally controllable luminaires.

Traditional approaches involve designing upwards from basic minimum standards of ambient lighting and applying any feature lighting on top, which requires high illuminances to cut through the ambient light. The alternative is to start with the feature lighting and user-controlled desk lights, building the visual hierarchy and adding ambient light only where it is needed. In this way, the feature lighting is an integral component of a holistic scheme, rather than an add-on that is likely to be lost in the first cost-saving exercise.

Right
Adjustable desk lamps in office environments are often referred to as 'task lamps', but different environments have different tasks and require different lighting. In this bar and restaurant, the principal visual task for the diners is to see their food and their companions. Staff behind the bar need to be able to clearly see the drinks and bar equipment, customers' faces, money tendered and the cash register.

Lighting for orientation

In many buildings, corridor spaces are depressing. They are vital for moving people around without disturbing their neighbours, but they are rarely inspiring or even comfortable spaces. Their usual location in the centre of a building affords little access to daylight or views to the outside. As they are often seen as simply an ancillary to the 'main' spaces, they seldom receive more than the minimum attention when it comes to lighting.

If a corridor had an analogy in nature, what would it be? In an open landscape, our field of view tends to encompass a luminous sky above and a ground below. The surrounding landscape generally occupies the vertical element of our view. So, there is generally brightness above, with a darker ground plane and vertical surfaces. This is not the typical corridor experience, where recessed downlights direct light at the floor, leaving the ceiling plane relatively dark.

In an exaggerated version of this visual experience, the typical corridor would resemble a cave, with daylight from outside lighting the floor and leaving the ceiling dark. In a cave, bright light signals daylight and an exit. Darkness is a sign of moving away from the outside and towards the unknown. Comparing a typically lit corridor with a cave allows us to understand why people have a natural tendency to want to move away from darkness and towards light – bright areas suggest openness, while dark ones suggest enclosure and lack of escape.

Being aware of this response means you can improve natural wayfinding within interior spaces without resorting to lots of signage. Ensuring that light levels increase towards exits and open spaces can help to draw people to these areas and away from darker service and staff ones.

Top right
In a cave, bright light signals an exit. View looking out of a beach cave at San Gregorio, California.

Bottom right
Two views of the same corridor space. The bright light at one end of the corridor is a much more enticing option than the gloom at the opposite end. Given no other clues about which way to turn, people are likely to feel most comfortable going towards the brighter space. In this case, the exit is round the brighter corner. However, this is by accident rather than design – an older lighting scheme using surface-mounted fluorescent luminaires remains in the bright section of corridor. It has not been designed deliberately to lead people towards the exit, but ably demonstrates the very different pattern of light produced by surface-mounted and recessed luminaires.

Left

A real-life application of an asymmetrical lighting scheme. This display corridor forms the entrance to an arts centre. The lighting designers worked closely with the architects to integrate the lighting into a series of very low spaces. The ceiling-recessed, fluorescent wall-wash luminaires provide excellent illumination of the display wall. This is the only electric lighting in the space and is all that is needed.

Below left

Even in daylight, nobody would feel comfortable entering this space were it not for the brightness at the end, which indicates an open space and potential safety.

Below right

The underground gallery in the Danish Design Centre, Copenhagen, is made far more inviting than it would otherwise be by the illuminated glass signage panel at the foot of the stair.

STEP BY STEP LIGHTING A CORRIDOR

Corridors are often among the least visually inspiring spaces in a building. In many buildings, corridors tend to be relegated to serving as simple functional routes, an unwelcome necessity required for circulation around the site. The lighting applied to such neglected spaces often reflects a similar lack of consideration for the end user, with the result that corridors can be depressing spaces. For these reasons, simple changes and improvements in the lighting of corridors can have a disproportionately significant impact on the visual experience

of a building. Dull and uninteresting corridors are great spaces for creative designers to carry out some thought experiments on how to use lighting to transform an area. In this example, no lighting calculation or modelling software was required. The alterations to the lit effect were all created in Photoshop as simple overlays of light and dark tints. Quick and easy photographic mock-ups such as this are very useful when demonstrating to clients the dramatic effects that can be achieved with simple lighting changes.

1 This unaltered photograph shows a corridor space in a university building. It is a clear example of a lighting scheme that has been laid out on the basis of providing even illumination of the floor. The whole space is illuminated by recessed downlights using compact fluorescent lamps. Although there is plenty of light in the space, it does not look or feel very bright. Part of the reason for the gloomy atmosphere is explained when we examine where the cones of light from the downlights meet the wall (most easily seen to the left of the blue noticeboard). The upper part of the wall receives no direct light from the downlights. The only light on the upper wall and the ceiling is reflected from the floor and lower wall. The large amount of dimly lit surface in our field of view has the psychological effect of lowering the height of the space, and increases the sense of enclosure.

2 Photo-editing software was used to experiment with alternative ways of lighting the space. Corridors are often treated as being symmetrical, with lighting centred to the space. In a narrow space like this there is no reason why it has to be centrally located, and creating asymmetrical lighting can be advantageous. In this image, the rooms on the right-hand side make up the perimeter of the building. Making this wall lighter alludes to the stronger natural light around the perimeter. Providing a strong light to the whole of this wall surface also gives a directional quality to the space. Travelling along the corridor in each direction gives a different visual experience. If applied consistently, this subtle effect can help visitors understand their location within the building.

3 The dark cave effect with a low, oppressive ceiling is largely created by the relative luminance of the ceiling. You can easily see the effect using Photoshop to add direct light on to the ceiling. In this corridor, the white ceiling panels reflect much more light than the coloured carpet. Therefore, making this surface appear bright takes a lot less light, directed at the ceiling, than the amount required to make the floor seem brightly illuminated. The ceiling panels would also be much more effective at bouncing light back on to the walls. In reality, the ceiling is not very high, so illuminating the ceiling so evenly would not be easy, but the effectiveness of uplighting it is easy to see.

4 Combining the lit wall with the uplit ceiling creates a very different atmosphere from the first image.

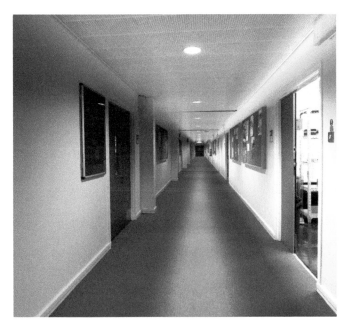 

5 This time the photograph has been manipulated to show how a set of narrow-beam downlights could create a very directional line of brightness that leads the viewer's eye to the end of the corridor. Despite this, the darkness at the end makes the corridor rather uninviting.

6 Even with dark walls and ceiling, a bright directional line and the light at the end of the corridor create a strong visual enticement to draw people through the space. It can be beneficial to break very long spaces down into smaller sections by modulating the lighting. In the same way that the bright area at the end of the corridor draws people towards it, lighting columns or creating a series of bright pools or colour changes can enliven a long walk through an airport or station.

Case study Wayfinding: Terminal 2F, Charles de Gaulle Airport, Paris, France

Lighting design and architecture Aéroports de Paris

The idea of using light as a natural form of wayfinding works at small and large scales. It was at the core of the architectural concepts for the design of the new Terminal 2F building at Charles de Gaulle Airport in Paris. The architects, Aéroports de Paris, created a mantra for the design of the terminal building: 'Follow the light.' This was how they foresaw people interacting with the architecture.

In the terminal building, there is a carefully orchestrated increase in natural light levels from check-in, through departures, security and finally on to the departure gates, which are flooded with natural light. The architects recognized that this well-planned control of light would allow them to guide departing passengers without having to rely on large signboards at every turn. This sophisticated use of light to aid wayfinding and orientation is rarely seen; most transport interchanges have to rely on a myriad of signs.

Various methods are employed throughout the terminal to control the amount of natural light that enters. The check-in space has very small

Above right
Passengers enter the terminal building through a glazed façade and cross over bridges that connect to the check-in area, which is dominated by the vast concrete arch that creates the terminal roof. Only small amounts of natural light penetrate this area, and it is filtered through rows of square roof-light apertures cast into the concrete. Brighter lines of natural light are created by narrow linear roof-lights that cut across the roof and lead towards the departure gates.

Right
Moving through the check-in area and towards the departure gates, the linear roof-lights begin to broaden, allowing more natural light into the building, but also creating a strong visual clue to the intended direction of travel.

areas of roof glazing, which are arranged as narrow slots that lead to the departure gates. The areas of glazing increase until, at the departure lounge, the whole roof structure is glazed. This amount of glass could have presented real problems of overheating and dazzle from direct sunlight. The architects have moderated the amount of sunlight with the addition of an external louvred screen. They call this 'the beetle's wing' and it covers most of the glazing, stopping short at the perimeter to allow clear views out to the airport apron beyond.

At night, the roof glazing takes on the blackness of the night sky. To overcome this effect, lighting is installed in the central spine of the roof structure. Some of the lighting is focused down to the lounge below, replicating the natural light direction. Other spotlights illuminate the white roof structure to visually brighten the ceiling against the dark sky.

Above right
As passengers approach the entrance to the departure gate, the heavy concrete roof peels away to leave a filigree structure of glass and steel. The bright ceiling provides a very strong pull towards the departure gate.

Right
The departure gate is completely glazed overhead. The roof is covered with an external louvre system that the architects refer to as 'the beetle's wing'. This prevents excessive light and heat penetration into the glazed structure. Although the glass wraps down to the floor slab, the louvres stop short and allow uninterrupted views out to the apron of the airport.

Avoiding glare

Shiny surfaces reflect light. This can be used to direct light to places we want it to go, but it can cause problems when the reflection is accidental and bright dazzling light is reflected towards the viewer.

There is no simple guaranteed solution to this problem, so designers need to be very aware of all the potential sources of glare and reflection. Glare problems are complex and cannot be avoided by designing on plan drawings; controlling glare requires the designer to constantly think in three dimensions and visualize the scene as the viewer will experience it.

All the projects in this book succeeded in avoiding glare problems, but some are particularly good examples, such as the St Mungo's Museum case study in this chapter (see following pages 100–1) and One Gyle Square in the next chapter (see pages 110–13).

Right
Specular reflections of light sources on glossy surfaces can be particularly problematic in situations where contrast levels are relatively low, such as in galleries and museums.

Exposure to light can be damaging to many fragile materials and this can be particularly problematic for museums and galleries. In order to protect sensitive objects, special conservation lighting standards are applied that restrict the amount of light that can be used to illuminate the exhibits. This leads to the common experience of very low light levels in museums and galleries, which can cause real difficulties for the lighting designer – any minor lighting problems, such as glare and distracting reflections, can be greatly exaggerated when general light levels are low.

In exhibition lighting, preventing glare greatly aids the visibility of exhibits lit to conservation lighting standards. Glare and sparkle from badly focused, poorly positioned or inappropriate luminaires provides the visual system with an excessively bright point of light by which to measure other lit surfaces. Our sense of 'brightness' has no in-built scale; it is purely a relative assessment. So, by comparison with an unshielded or reflected light source, any exhibits illuminated to conservation lighting levels appear to be very dim and gloomy.

Glare can be a particular problem when working with exhibits that are behind glass. Minimizing distracting reflections requires a great deal of careful thought, planning, experimentation and, above all, a lot of time spent perfecting the focus of each light source during commissioning.

We think of glass as a transparent medium. However, this relies on certain conditions. When the objects and surfaces beyond the glass are more luminous than any reflection in the glass, we can see through the glass. When the reflections in the glass are more luminous than the objects beyond, it can be difficult to see through the glass. This 'veiling reflection' disrupts our view through the glass. This effect can be clearly seen in any street at night. As we walk along the street, we are able to see into rooms that have internal lights switched on. It is dark outside and little light is reflected off the window glass, so we can see into the room beyond. During the day, the same room could be much brighter because of daylight streaming through the windows. However, the observer on the street outside receives far more light reflected from the bright sky and so finds it difficult to see into the room. Note that this effect has nothing to do with the difference in light levels during the day and night; it is about the relative intensity on each side of the glass. If we stand inside the lit room at night and look at the window, we are likely to see little more than ourselves and the room reflected in the glass.

In less extreme situations, distracting reflections can be created when there is a significant contrast between the bright points of a reflected light and the background they are seen against. This is particularly apparent with point sources such as spotlights, but can also apply to linear ones such as fluorescents. These problems can often be avoided by repositioning the light sources, the reflective surface or the viewer. People often unconsciously move position slightly to try to avoid reflections interfering with their view. This repositioning cannot always be achieved, so other solutions sometimes have to be found to deal with reflective surfaces such as glass.

Rather than directing concentrated beams of light from small sources such as spotlights towards the reflective surface, it is possible to light an object indirectly by bouncing the light off diffusing surfaces such as walls and ceilings. With skill and thoughtful design, it is possible to minimize the contrast between the brightest and darkest surfaces reflected in the glass. With minimal contrast, it is much easier for the visual system to see through any reflection in the glass to the objects beyond. This technique can be adapted to work for a seemingly impossible lighting task (see the case study on the following pages).

Case study Low light gallery, St Mungo's Museum of Religious Life and Art, Glasgow, UK

Lighting design Kevan Shaw Lighting Design
Architect Page and Park Architects

Glasgow's St Mungo's Museum of Religious Life and Art has a display in its low light gallery that consists of a set of small prints by Albrecht Dürer, which are shown in shallow desk cases angled towards the viewer. On the wall above the prints hang two paintings by William Blake. All these items are very light-sensitive and the light levels need to be tightly controlled. Some of the problems involved in providing glare-free lighting for the display can be seen in the schematic cross section of the space (opposite left).

Because of the tilt of the display cases, any luminaires mounted above them would be reflected directly into the eyes of the viewer and obscure his or her view of the prints. If the light sources were moved further back from the wall to

avoid this problem, a shadow of the viewer would be cast over the display as they approached it and the shallow angle of lighting would create ceiling reflections in the glazed paintings above the cases. Wall-mounted spotlights could avoid reflecting the light into the viewer's face, but would create patches of light on the opposite wall and could also cast shadows of the case edges across the exhibits.

To solve this problem, Kevan Shaw Lighting Design worked closely with Page and Park Architects to create a very diffused light that was reflected from several surfaces before it reached the exhibits. This gave an even and non-directional light that would allow very close examination of the small prints without the

Below
Lighting the paintings on the end wall, with glass display cases below, presented one of the greatest challenges for the lighting designers. The specially created illuminated void above provides the diffused lighting required.

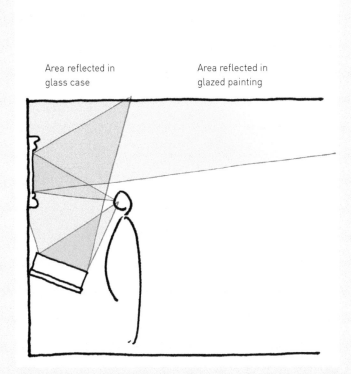

Area reflected in glass case

Area reflected in glazed painting

exhibits being in shadow. A high colour rendering dimmable fluorescent was mounted in a deep coffer above the display. A custom reflector was designed to provide an even spread of light over all the internal surfaces of the coffer. The coffer was sized to represent the area reflected in the display cases, and because there was almost no contrast variation over that area, the reflection in the case top was featureless and did not cause a distraction.

Rather than direct illumination coming from a series of small light sources, which would have meant a large luminance contrast between the source and its surroundings, the whole of the coffer and upper walls became the light source. The luminance is much lower and does not seem unbalanced compared to the low conservation light levels on the exhibits themselves.

This solution was very successful with these two-dimensional objects, but would not work so well for three-dimensional or textural exhibits as, without any directional quality to the light, they would lose their depth.

Above left

This sketch section through the gallery shows the lighting problem that had to be solved. For a viewer looking at a wall-mounted painting, the glass will reflect a large proportion of the ceiling area (marked in blue). Any spotlights mounted in this area would cause distracting reflections in the painting. The normal solution is to position the luminaires closer to the painting where they will not be reflected. However, in this instance, an angled desk case is mounted below the painting, and its surface reflects all the soffit area, where the luminaires used to light the painting would normally be positioned. Furthermore, luminaires in the blue zone that were directed at the desk cases would cast shadows of the viewer over the case. Given that this is a low light gallery and all the exhibits are displayed with illuminance levels of around 50 lux, any reflections of spotlight luminaires would present such a high contrast that the reflection would make the exhibits unviewable.

Above right

The lighting designers devised a custom lighting solution that provided an excellent quality of light, at just the right levels, for both the wall display and the objects in the desk cases. The solution was to reduce the contrast with a dimmable linear fluorescent lamp mounted in a concealed cove above the display area. A custom-designed reflector ensures that the whole of the white-painted ceiling void is evenly illuminated with no dark patches. This turns the whole cavity into a luminaire that produces a very soft, inter-reflected light. Although the ceiling void is reflected in the desk cases, it presents a low-luminance, contrast-free reflection that does not interfere with the view through the glass. The exhibits are illuminated by light that is reflected from several surfaces, and this creates a diffused, shadow-free light that is ideal for close examination of the desk cases.

7. Lighting for architecture

The best lighting for the users of a building is often light that is focused on the surfaces around them. Without controlled light to illuminate the surfaces that make up the built environment, we cannot begin to feel that we understand our surroundings. When it comes to architecture, how do we decide what to light, and how do we achieve it without visually intrusive equipment?

Ambient lighting

Ambient lighting exists in all lit environments. As designers, we rely on reflections from lit surfaces to illuminate any areas that are not directly lit by luminaires. The inter-reflection of ambient light helps to smooth out the contrast between direct and indirect illumination and ambient light can soften shadows. Controlling it is an important element in any project, but sometimes we may choose to use indirect or ambient lighting as the principal means of illumination. This can be especially useful for very large volumes.

Left and opposite
At 1.2 km long, the departures area of Terminal 4 at Madrid Barajas Airport is vast. Any traditional downlighting scheme would have led to thousands of pinpricks of light peppering the soffit, and would have produced contrast issues between the bright luminaires and the unlit soffit. Lighting designers Speirs and Major Associates worked with the architects (Richard Rogers Partnership with Estudio Lamela) to produce a lighting scheme that provided a good level of ambient lighting at ground level while also illuminating the architecture in a sympathetic fashion. High-power metal halide luminaires are focused upwards on to proprietary mirrored reflectors, which are shaped to provide a very even spread of light at ground level without glare problems. The uplighting is deliberately allowed to spill beyond the reflectors to illuminate the bamboo-slat soffit and the white discs that sit below roof lights and diffuse natural light during the day. This arrangement ensures that the quality of diffused daylight is replicated at night and that the roof lights do not become black when the sun sets. The uplighting also reduces the contrast between the reflectors and their surroundings to minimize any potential glare problems.

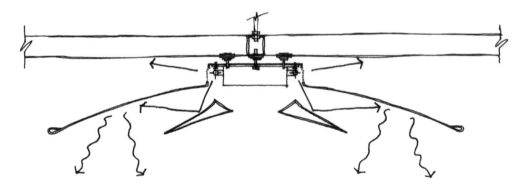

Above and left

On the lower floors of the new Terminal 4 at Madrid Barajas Airport, large open areas are illuminated with custom-designed indirect luminaires that create a glare-free reflected light and act as a soffit. The luminaires are based around a modified version of a proprietary, recessed circular T5 fluorescent downlight. This is set into a large white dish, while a suspended doughnut-shaped baffle below the downlight prevents a direct view of the lamp and bounces light back on to the reflector dish.

Left and below
To prevent excessive contrast making a well-lit space feel like a dark cave, the lighting designers for Madrid Barajas Airport, Speirs and Major Associates, used simple CAD models to assess the best finish for the ceiling void above the luminaires. The bottom image shows less contrast.

Below
Gallery lighting is frequently concerned with picking out small objects from the background. This requires good contrast between the object and the ambient light. In this example, the lighting designers provided the ultimate lighting flexibility for this gallery by specifying a steel soffit and spotlight luminaires with magnetic bases. This allows the luminaires to be positioned anywhere on the soffit to suit different exhibitions.

Accent lighting

People, like magpies, like shiny things. Our visual system is naturally drawn to the brightest objects in our field of view. There is no definitive reason why this may be so, but it is certainly true that brightly lit shapes, with good levels of contrast, are much easier to identify than ones that are dimly lit, with shadow-free illumination. It could be as simple as that – a scene can be understood more quickly if we examine the brightest areas first. Whatever the reason, the effect is real and it inadvertently produces the sense that bright equals important.

This gives the lighting designer the power to establish a visual hierarchy by controlling the brightness of each part of a scene. Accents can be created not just with increased light levels, but with changes in the direction or colour of light. They can be used subtly to draw people towards light areas, or to reveal detail that may be difficult to see. As in the case study for One Gyle Square (see pages 110–13), accent lighting can even be used to help describe architectural form.

Far left
A single spotlight picks out a statue in Notre-Dame, Paris. The angle and high contrast of the spotlight enhance the three-dimensional modelling of the figure, increasing its visual importance.

Left
Accent lighting can be used to reveal detail that may not be immediately obvious. The shadow of this small sculpture reveals the delicate filigree structure of the leaves, a feature that was lost in the general ambient light of the room.

Below
By tightly controlling the intensity and spread of light, we can control where people look. The lighting of a suite of exhibition spaces in the Statens Museum for Kunst, Copenhagen, frames a clear progression of views from one room to the next.

Right
The deliberately restrained light levels in this lobby area contrast with the strong uplighting that highlights the arched doorway, drawing visitors into the main space beyond. Lighting for orientation and wayfinding is explored on pages 92–7.

Case study One Gyle Square, Edinburgh, UK

Lighting design FOTO-MA

Architect Michael Laird Architects

Minimally decorated architectural spaces are among the most challenging to illuminate. In spaces with little other decorative detail, lighting can become a dominant visual statement whether you intend it to or not. The designer has to apply great skill to produce a lighting solution that reinforces the architect's vision while providing appropriate illumination levels in the correct locations. For a successful outcome, the design team must have a clear vision of what they are trying to achieve and how it can be done. The architects and designers must work collaboratively and value each other's input to be able to find effective solutions, since the visual impact of spaces can easily be destroyed by grids of downlights, ventilation grilles and other services. The lighting designer has to work with

the architect to find the best lighting approaches that will get the light where it is needed without disturbing the visual balance of uninterrupted plaster surfaces. Ill-considered lighting can break the magic of minimal spaces by penetrating the pristine surfaces with grids, shapes and patterns of luminaires, and also by placing luminaires without considering the accidental pattern of illumination on all the adjacent surfaces.

In illuminating the reception space for this office development, the designers created a lighting scheme that belies the skill and complexity involved with a look of effortless simplicity. The lit effect is not produced by highly technical equipment, but with simple techniques applied to a very high standard.

Opposite
The external view was a key consideration in this design. The cluster of three 35 W metal halide downlights on the exterior canopy carefully mirrors the three on the inside, creating continuity between inside and outside. The luminaires chosen have very narrow, 10° beams to avoid creating unsightly scallops on the adjacent wall surfaces. The concealed cove lighting that provides ambient light within the reception area continues up the vertical face and over the top edge of the atrium wall, to create the illusion of a massive geometric block hovering within the entrance. The lighting is pared back to the elements that provide the subtle visual statement of the entrance.

Above left
Direct light was required to make the reception desk stand out within the entrance area and to provide a good quality of light for staff and visitors. Rather than introduce a new visual element with a line of luminaires recessed into the plaster ceiling, the lighting designers incorporated tiny spotlights into a decorative stainless-steel feature band. These downlights are fibre-optic, which means the luminaires are physically very small and the light source can be located in a remote location where maintenance will be easier. Using fibre-optic luminaires with a remote light source meant that, once installed, no access into the stainless-steel band would be required for maintenance.

Above right
Much of the ambient light in the space is produced by indirect light from concealed linear fluorescent luminaires mounted in the cove that runs round the whole soffit. Ceiling-recessed downlights using circular T5 fluorescent lamps create a subtle visual pathway that leads visitors past the reception desk and links the reception area to the corridor beyond.

Left

A lighting cove runs all round the lowered soffit over the reception desk. The slot emanates an intense white light that manages to visually dislocate the weight of the lowered soffit from the side walls. The result is a plane that appears to float weightlessly over the reception. Lighting coves are common features in many kinds of architecture, but they are frequently done very badly. Most attempts at cove lighting end up with splashes of bright light interspersed with dark bands. It takes great skill to produce a cove or slot that is as evenly illuminated as the one shown here. It is often thought that simply laying out a line of linear fluorescent luminaires end to end will create a perfectly even line of light – it will not. In this project, the cove conceals linear T5 fluorescent lamps, which are overlapped by a minimum of 70 mm to ensure there are no dark sections in the line.

Below

Diagram illustrating the overlapping placement of lamps in the cove.

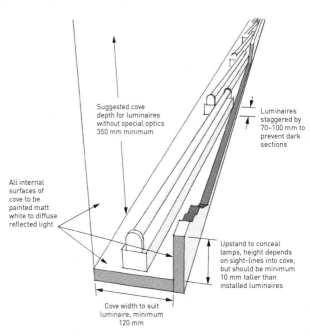

Suggested cove depth for luminaires without special optics 350 mm minimum

Luminaires staggered by 70–100 mm to prevent dark sections

All internal surfaces of cove to be painted matt white to diffuse reflected light

Upstand to conceal lamps, height depends on sight-lines into cove, but should be minimum 10 mm taller than installed luminaires

Cove width to suit luminaire, minimum 120 mm

Case study Sheikh Zayed bin Sultan Al-Nahyan Mosque (The Grand Mosque), Abu Dhabi, UAE

Lighting design Speirs and Major Associates

Left

There are two open prayer halls behind the main prayer hall that open directly on to the courtyard beyond. The designers wanted to create a unifying feel in these spaces, with luminous walls washed from a perimeter slot at high level. The ceilings in the open prayer halls are 11.3 metres above floor level, so the wall-wash solution uses different luminaires and a different slot detail to create the same effect as in the prayer hall. The luminous vertical walls approach was repeated in external lobbies and colonnades; each type of space required a different, carefully crafted lighting treatment to create a continuity of lit effect. The open prayer halls have wind catchers on the roof; these are capped with decorative open fretwork grilles at ceiling level. These grilles, and some smaller decorative ones, are backlit to provide additional lighting for the space. The backlighting to the fretwork changes colour over the course of the day to represent external daylight conditions. The colour gradually shifts from the crisp white daylight feel of this image to a subtle midnight blue in the evening.

When higher light levels are required, a small number of recessed downlights are switched on (as seen here) to provide direct light at ground level.

Opposite

Although the ambient light levels at ground level are not high, the use of strong wall washing to create luminous vertical surfaces gives the perception of a space that is much brighter than would be measured by a lux meter. The lighting is dynamic and changes depending on activities inside the building and the time of day.

The Grand Mosque in Abu Dhabi is a project that overflows with incredible statistics. The building consists of a series of single-level public spaces that cover over 22,000 square metres. It has capacity for 40,000 worshippers. But for all the complexity and vast scale of the project, the design approach taken for the interior lighting was deliberately restrained and respectful. However, the simple palette of lighting approaches that were used required some complex and accurately crafted installations to create the perfect results.

The main prayer hall is the principal space in the complex and is the most ornately decorated of the public spaces. The hall is large enough to accommodate over 7,000 worshippers and is topped by three domes, including the largest dome of its kind, which stands at 85 metres. All the surfaces of this vast space are intricately decorated, from the world's largest handwoven carpet (5,627 square metres) on the floor to the inlaid marble walls and carved plasterwork of the ceiling. The hall is a visual feast of decoration.

With this in mind, Speirs and Major Associates made a conscious decision to avoid creating another pattern of holes in the ornate plaster ceiling by installing the lighting there. Despite the vast proportions of the space, the decision was taken to use the vertical surfaces as the principal 'light givers'. The whole hall was envisioned as being a luminous object with light seeming to emanate from the walls. For the designers, it was important that the light was as even as possible over the full height of the outer walls so that the whole surface became luminous. In more modest spaces, this can easily be achieved with good-quality wall-wash luminaires that are specifically designed for such a purpose. However, this is not a typical architectural space, and the 22.5-metre height of the walls precluded the effective use of such luminaires, which might have managed to light only the top 5 metres of the wall effectively.

The other self-imposed restriction was that the designers were determined to position the luminaires in such a way that they would not be seen from any normal viewing position at ground level. The solution involved the use of a 1.1-metre-deep perimeter slot to conceal the

0° tilt (parallel to wall)

16 metres

5° tilt (parallel to wall)

10° tilt (parallel to wall)

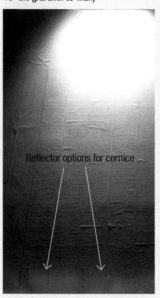

Reflector options for cornice

20° tilt (parallel to wall)

Above

The only way to ensure the best visual results for the wall wash was to build a full-size mock-up. The vertical wall was modelled on the ground plane to allow lux level measurements to be taken and so that the luminaires were easy to reach for adjustments. Earlier computer modelling suggested that the idea of creating a wall wash from two different sets of luminaires could work in principle, but the physical tests were required to determine the details. Different tilt angles were tested, measured and photographed before the best option was chosen. For the final installation, both the wall-wash luminaires for the upper wall and the spotlight luminaires for the lower wall were specified with a tilt angle of 2.5°. This angle was preset in the factory so that every luminaire would be exactly the same. The cornice-level gold and silver reflectors seen in these images were replaced with white marble to produce a softer, untinted reflection.

Below left

The mock-up was created on a theatre stage. The installation was turned on its side to make the testing easier, with the stage floor representing the vertical wall. The test set-up allowed for the adjustment of the spacing between luminaires, the distance between luminaires and the lit surface, and the tilt angle of the luminaires. This image shows the testing of four very narrow-beam spotlights fitted with linear spread lenses. These luminaires were used to illuminate the lower part of the wall.

Each narrow spotlight was partnered with a luminaire with wall-wash reflector that was used to illuminate the upper part of the wall. One of the wall-wash luminaires, switched off for the test, is in the centre of the image. The luminaires were to be concealed in a slot above the ceiling; the scaffold bars on the ground represented the ceiling plane in the test.

Below right

This photograph, taken during construction, shows how well the wall wash illuminates the floral-patterned inlaid-marble walls.

Section through light cove at suspended ceiling scale 1:10

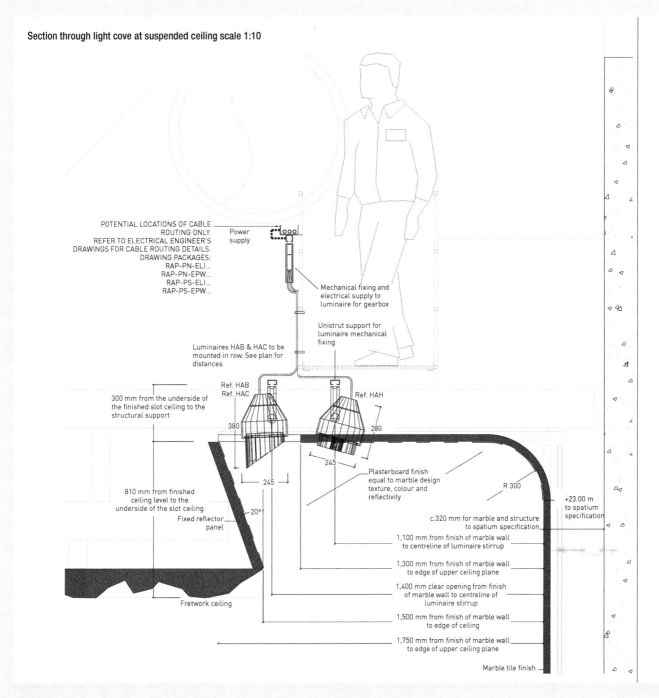

POTENTIAL LOCATIONS OF CABLE
ROUTING ONLY.
REFER TO ELECTRICAL ENGINEER'S
DRAWINGS FOR CABLE ROUTING DETAILS.
DRAWING PACKAGES:
RAP-PN-ELI...
RAP-PN-EPW...
RAP-PS-ELI...
RAP-PS-EPW...

Power supply

Mechanical fixing and
electrical supply to
luminaire for gearbox

Unistrut support for
luminaire mechanical
fixing

Luminaires HAB & HAC to be
mounted in row. See plan for
distances

Ref. HAB
Ref. HAC

Ref. HAH

300 mm from the underside of
the finished slot ceiling to the
structural support

380

280

245

810 mm from finished
ceiling level to the
underside of the slot ceiling

245

Plasterboard finish
equal to marble design
texture, colour and
reflectivity

R 300

20°

Fixed reflector
panel

c.320 mm for marble and structure
to spatium specification

+23.00 m
to spatium
specification

1,100 mm from finish of marble wall
to centreline of luminaire stirrup

1,300 mm from finish of marble wall
to edge of upper ceiling plane

1,400 mm clear opening from finish
of marble wall to centreline of
luminaire stirrup

1,500 mm from finish of marble wall
to edge of ceiling

1,750 mm from finish of marble wall
to edge of upper ceiling plane

Fretwork ceiling

Marble tile finish

Above

Despite the scale of the mosque, the construction of the lighting slot had to be millimetre-perfect. The lighting is maintained from above and a maintenance walkway runs above the ceiling level. The luminaire to the right in this partial section drawing is a special-use spotlight, which is directed into the hall and is only used to provide additional light at ground level for television broadcasts. The pairs of wall-wash luminaires are on the left of the drawing and face towards the vertical wall. As it is possible for people to see into the slot when they are standing close to the wall, the detailing was carefully considered. The materials used for the decorative wall are run into the slot and a gentle curve wraps the vertical surface round to create a soffit without introducing a visible line. The wall-wash luminaires are actually centred over the edge of the ceiling, which makes it possible to look into the slot from ground level without being blinded by the luminaires. This means some light from the luminaires is cut off by the soffit line. This light was put to use by creating a carefully angled reflector panel that reflects light back into the slot to ensure there are no visible scallops of light from the various luminaires.

luminaires, and a careful layering of light sources to create the desired effect. Extensive testing proved that the full 23.6 metres of the side walls (including the slot) could be evenly illuminated from a series of luminaires mounted only 1.5 metres from the wall surface.

The lighting designers' instinct was that it might be just about feasible to make this solution work, but not with proprietary wall-wash lighting systems. A solution was found by testing different luminaire combinations and positions using a virtual model built in DIALux lighting design software. However, computer modelling was only one part of the testing, as the results could not effectively describe what the lighting would really look like. Given the scale of the task and the very small space available to work with, it was essential to produce a full-size mock-up so that the lit effect could be properly assessed visually, and precise measurements of the aiming angles and spacing of the luminaires could be made. The task of setting up the mock-up was not easy. There are not many suitable spaces with a large enough area of flat surface and complete blackout facilities that can be used for lighting

tests. In the end, the tests were carried out on the stage of a large theatre that was empty between productions.

The full-scale mock-up allowed the designers to check how closely the results from the computer modelling matched the measured results from the real luminaires. Minor changes were made as a result, and the designers were confident they could detail a solution that would work for the final installation.

Above
Although it is possible to see into the perimeter slot from the edges of the room, the wall-wash luminaires are positioned in such a way that they cannot be seen from any normal viewing position at ground level. The dark dots in the image are special luminaires used only for television broadcasts.

Opposite
The lighting design includes direct lighting in areas where higher light levels are required, such as providing light for worshippers who wish to study the copies of the Qur'an located between the column clusters. The wall-wash treatment is the principal lighting for the floral walls, but they also contain inlaid glass patterns that are backlit at certain times of day to suggest daylight filtering through the coloured glass. As this decorative wall is actually several metres from the outer skin of the building, the backlighting is provided by fluorescent battens mounted behind the glass.

Below
Many lighting schemes only
address illumination of horizontal
surfaces, such as the ground plane
or work surfaces. However, for
the users of a space, the vertical
surfaces often make up a much
larger proportion of their field of
view. Good lighting design must
consider the vertical surfaces in a
lit environment, and ensure that
any light that falls on the vertical
planes is intentional and forms part
of a balanced approach to light
throughout the space.

Lighting vertical surfaces

Much of the lighting we experience in architecture has been designed on a set of architectural plan drawings. Lighting layouts often seem to have been arranged to create an even amount of light on the ground from an even distribution of holes in the ceiling.

However, we do not experience architecture in plan; we experience architectural space in three dimensions, with vertical surfaces usually making up the largest proportion of our field of view. Sadly, most lighting designs seem to ignore this fact and any light falling on vertical surfaces is an accidental effect of the placement of luminaires designed to light the ground or horizontal work surfaces. This situation is not helped by the many lighting codes and standards that focus on quantifying only the light that falls on to horizontal surfaces.

Nevertheless, an experienced designer recognizes that in most architectural spaces, the visual perception of brightness can be greatly enhanced by providing light to the vertical surfaces. In many smaller areas, such as corridors, it is possible to adequately illuminate the whole space with light directed only at the vertical surfaces. This approach is unlikely to succeed in larger spaces, but it can form an important element within a larger set of techniques used to illuminate a space.

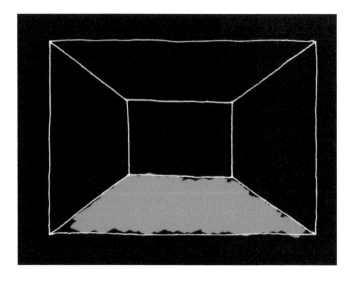
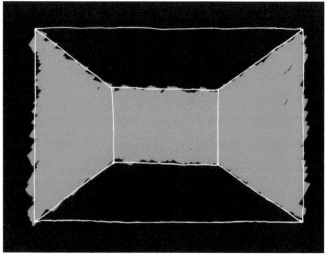

Integrating light with architecture

Any great lighting scheme must respect and respond to the architecture it inhabits and illuminates. But it is also the case that great lighting cannot simply be bolted on to a space; it has to be integrated with the architectural and interior design. Light is a revealer of space, and therefore has to be seen as part of an overall spatial design in which lighting and physical structures work together to achieve the very best visual experience.

It is true that most lighting is not designed in this way. It is often treated as one of the building services along with heating, ventilation, and electrical and data cabling – something that is necessary but should ultimately be kept out of sight lest it spoil the view of the space.

Nevertheless, there are design teams who work together to create the best visual experience. With respect for, and appreciation of, each other's skills and opinions, they can create magical spaces where light sources are secreted into the architecture to create spatial designs that seem to produce an effortless glow from within. Lighting design should not be about luminaires and technology; it is really about light and surface. The following case study of Morimoto Restaurant by Focus Lighting exemplifies this approach.

Left
Rather than introduce visually intrusive pendants or surface-mounted luminaires into this space in the Museum of World Cultures, Gothenburg, Sweden, the lighting is integrated into the architecture with luminaires set into stair risers and a glowing bulkhead below the glazed wall. Architecture by Brisac Gonzalez Architects, lighting design by Speirs and Major Associates.

Case study Morimoto Restaurant, Philadelphia, USA

Lighting design Focus Lighting
Architect Karim Rashid

Morimoto Restaurant was conceived as a unique dining experience where diners are contained within a room whose walls are seen as a kinetic sculpture. The qualities of these sculpted walls became an important visual feature for the lighting designers. Paul Gregory of Focus Lighting described them as being 'like a painting' and saw that they would 'provide the frame for the patrons' first view of this beautiful space'.

Gregory's way of visualizing a space is influenced by a background in theatrical stage lighting. He has described this project in terms of 'scenes' – the sequence of visual experiences that greet patrons as they arrive outside the restaurant, enter through the front doors, glimpse the dining room, see its full splendour as they

are shown to their table, and then settle into the intimacy of their booth.

Given this carefully considered and dramatic approach to lighting, the designers always work hard to make the light set the perfect scene and tell the story they want to convey. This takes a huge amount of skill and experience, but also a willingness to experiment and refine ideas until they are perfect. As part of the theatrical approach taken with this project, much of the lighting equipment is concealed from view with the lit surfaces becoming the visible sources of light.

In describing the space, the designers say that 'the walls are the largest architectural and lighting element within the space and appear to be glowing from within. The walls emit a warm

Above
With the wall-grazing lighting dimmed down low, the undulating plaster takes on a luxurious golden glow. The deep blue of the backlit partition walls is complementary to the gold, and the two colours enhance each other to produce a sophisticated harmony. The intimacy of the booths is heightened by the dimmable electric candles mounted on the green glass tables. It seems as though the candles are illuminating the space, but they are supplemented by narrow-beam directional downlights, which light the tables from above. The downlights are dimmed to match the colour quality of the candles and enhance the sense of intimate dining by candlelight.

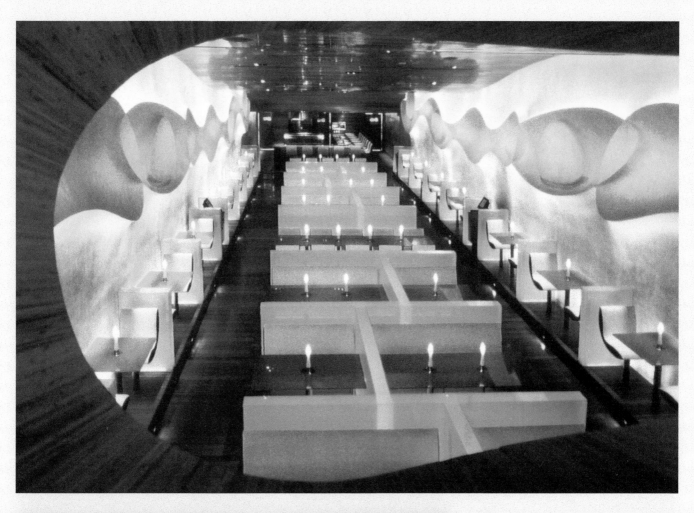

Above

The layout of the dining room. Lighting slots run between the perimeter seating booths and the plaster walls. The undulating timber soffit stops short of the walls, creating slots to downlight the plaster walls from above. Pale blue in the partitions and bright side walls creates a dining atmosphere for daylight hours.

Left

The huge palette of colours available from the colour-changing LED luminaires allows the lighting to be adjusted for special occasions such as Valentine's Day. The attention to detail in the lighting of the plaster walls can be seen by the almost complete lack of light spilling on to the timber soffit from the ground-level uplights, and the invisibility of the lamps in the high-level slot.

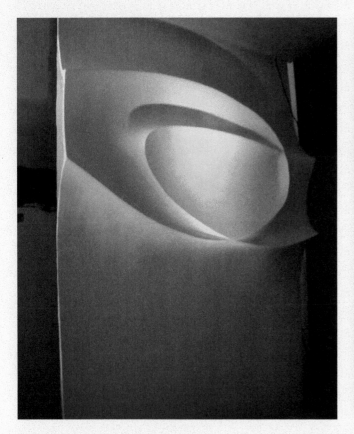

glow that engulfs the space and provides a pleasing warm tone to the patrons' faces.' This almost magical lighting is achieved by creating a very narrow slot along the edge of a raised floor area into which a continuous run of narrow-beam lamps is placed to graze light up the wall. The slot is mirrored at high level with lamps placed above the undulating timber soffit. This kind of detail can be achieved only through careful integration of lighting design, architectural design and interior design. Everything has to come together to make such a bold design idea work well.

A physical mock-up was required to ensure that every detail was tuned to perfection, and to allow the whole design team to see why this detailing was critical. The 3 metres wide by 5 metres high sample panel allowed the designers to determine the spacing between lamps and the size of slot that would provide the best illumination of the wall. It also allowed them to determine exactly where to locate the single narrow-beam spotlights that very subtly pick out the outer surface of the sculptured shapes.

This attention to detail and use of mock-ups extended to the treatment of the etched glass partitions between seating booths, which were originally conceived by the architect as being single sheets of glass. The lighting designers proposed a double-walled construction, to provide space for internal lighting that would give the partitions an ethereal glow. Using iColor Cove, a colour-changing linear LED luminaire, gave them the option of making the partitions glow with any colour they wanted. The cost of this element could have prevented its adoption. However, another mock-up created by the lighting designers allowed the client to see exactly what could be achieved, and approval was immediate.

The colour choices for the partition walls were vital to maintain the ambience of the restaurant, and a carefully considered palette was used to enhance the dining experience. Colours and general light levels change slowly to create an appropriate atmosphere for dining at different times of day. The lighting is so critical to the look and feel of the restaurant that it is impossible to imagine the space without it. The light is truly an integral part of the architecture.

Above left
The full-size mock-up of a plaster wall shows how it would look if it was lit only from ceiling luminaires.

Above right
The addition of the grazing light from the concealed slots changes the solid plaster into a seemingly luminous surface. This is a remarkable transformation and is not easily appreciated without a physical demonstration such as this.

Divider wall LED uplight

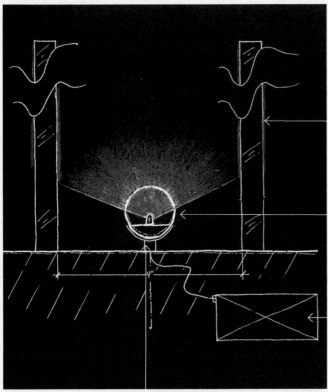

12 mm sandblasted glass

Colour-changing LED strip with mounting channel to backlight glass enclosure

LED transformer/ control module located in basement

100 mm min opening

Wall uplight

180 mm platform for side wall seating

Finished floor

Undulating wall

Metal shutter to provide glare control (hinged for lamp access)

Par 30 lamp with accessory holder and hex-cell louvre

Linear socket strip (150 mm on centre)

Above
The partitions during construction without their capping glass. The linear LED uplight can be seen in the base of the partition. The carefully considered choice of glass provides the gradation of light from the bright band at the base, fading towards the top of the partition.

Above left
Sketch detail of the lighting for the etched glass partitions. Various glass options were tested in a physical mock-up before the required level of translucency was selected.

Below left
Sketch detail showing the slot-mounted uplights to the plaster walls. Some things can only be determined by doing – all the critical dimensions, including the distance between lamp and wall, the distance between individual lamps and the size of the slot opening were worked out with the use of the full-size mock-up. The light source used was a dimmable mains voltage tungsten halogen reflector lamp, which is cheap, and easy to source and replace. Although these lamps have a relatively short life, they are always slightly dimmed, which can significantly extend the life of incandescent lamps.

8. The design process

The lighting design process is not always easy to define as it varies for every project, but general principles are true for most cases. Every design project should begin with a brief. This may be created by the client or the designer may be employed to carry out a feasibility study that will include defining a brief for the lighting project. The design process is often iterative with great leaps forward followed by redesign of some areas that prove to be problematic, but the general movement is towards more and more detail until the whole project can be defined in a way that allows a contractor to supply and install exactly what the designer wants.

Construction projects that are larger than very small domestic ones are designed by a team of design specialists.

The lead designer is usually the architect or landscape architect and the project is therefore often defined by the scope and work stages of a typical architectural contract. Other members of the design team need the architectural information, in order to work from it, but they also have to feed their designs to the lead designers to ensure that their work is properly incorporated into the project and that clashes are avoided. This means the lighting designer is working behind the architectural team, but also trying to stay ahead of the next stage of work.

There are as many models for a successful lighting project as there are projects. The diagrams on these pages show typical routes for the design of architectural lighting.

Right
Design is rarely a linear process. Each stage becomes progressively more detailed, and this often uncovers difficulties with the original proposal or better solutions that require the designer to revisit an earlier work stage. This is not a case of going backwards, but an important iterative method for improving and refining design ideas.

Design proposals at concept stage can alter the scope of the project, and the brief

Concepts may need to be revised after testing at design development stage

Detailed investigation may identify areas to be revisited

Compare results with the brief for reference

```
┌─────────────────────┐
│   Lighting brief     │
└─────────────────────┘
           ↓
┌─────────────────────┐
│  Lighting concepts   │
└─────────────────────┘
           ↓
┌─────────────────────┐
│    Scheme design     │
└─────────────────────┘
           ↓
┌─────────────────────┐
│    Detail design     │
└─────────────────────┘
           ↓
┌─────────────────────┐
│    Construction      │
│   administration     │
└─────────────────────┘
           ↓
┌─────────────────────┐
│     Final focus      │
└─────────────────────┘
           ↓
┌─────────────────────┐
│     Completion       │
└─────────────────────┘
```

ARCHITECTURAL WORK STAGES   LIGHTING DESIGN WORK STAGES

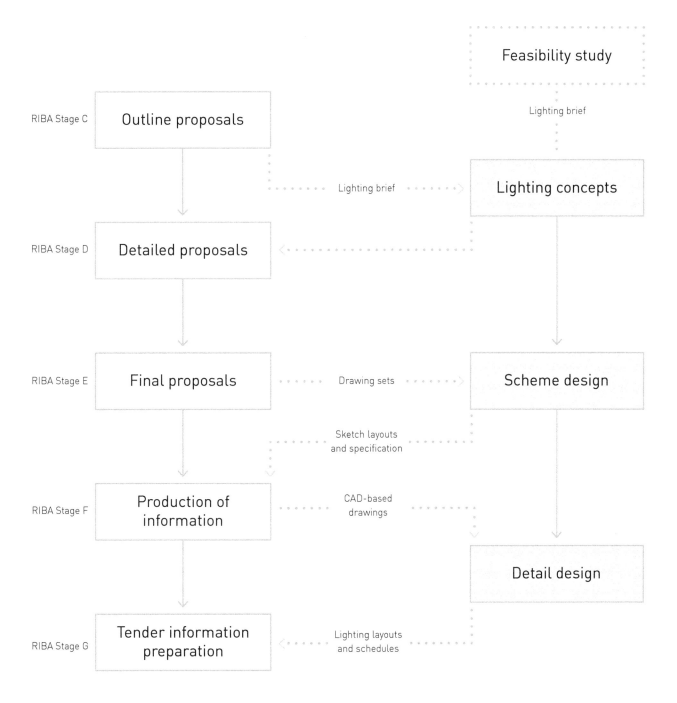

Above

Illustration of one pattern of working with a UK-based architectural team. In the UK, architects and many other designers usually work on a contract that is based on the 'Plan of Work Stages' published by the Royal Institute of British Architects (RIBA). There are contractual stages before and after those shown here, but this shows how a lighting design process may mesh

with the architectural design. It is increasingly common for the lighting designer to collaborate with the architect at the early stages of a project to secure the desired look, and lighting elements often influence architectural decisions. However, lighting requires surfaces to illuminate. Therefore, documentation of the lighting design will generally follow the architectural design.

Design is an iterative process and at each stage, lighting will be based on the drawing information supplied by the architect. In turn, lighting information will be fed back to the rest of the design team to modify and inform the next stage of the design process.

Researching the project

An important requirement in any project is to clearly define the scope of the work and what the client needs and expects. However, clients and other design team professionals are rarely lighting or architectural professionals, and may not know what they need. For an existing building, the designer needs to talk to the client at length about how it is currently used, not only at different times of day, but throughout the week and the year. Who uses the building (staff and visitors) and what are the typical hours of use? How might this change in the future? How is the lighting currently switched and controlled, and who has access to the controls? It is also good to know who maintains the lighting and how often it is maintained, as this can inform the best choice of equipment and mounting locations.

Analysis of needs

Where there is an expectation of energy savings, accurate data must be collected and compared. Using information about the existing building, its typical pattern of use and the current lighting equipment, it is possible to estimate the running and maintenance costs. This can help to identify any particular areas where significant improvements can be made. This information is also useful in helping the client to understand the differences between the existing and proposed schemes.

Below
For visual designers, drawing and sketching can be a valuable method for understanding a design problem or project site. In principle, CAD can provide unparalleled accuracy, but hand drawing gives the designer a tangible interaction through the marks made on the paper. This physical contact leaves a kind of muscle memory of the project, making it easier to visualize and recreate the scene in the mind when imagining suitable lighting approaches.

Outline proposal stage

The outline proposal stage, often called concept stage by lighting designers, is usually one of the most creative parts of the design process. Also, if the project includes a thorough feasibility stage, the general lighting approach has probably been established by this point. An important feature of the concept stage is communicating the lighting proposals to the client and the rest of the design team. If you can clearly demonstrate what the proposed approach will do, and how it will be achieved, it will make it much easier to gain the assistance you will need from the other members of the design team.

Effective communication of lighting ideas requires clear and engaging visuals, and these can take time to perfect. On smaller projects, this stage often accounts for a large amount of the total design time. This should not be seen as a problem. Taking the time to work up concept ideas to a level where they can be presented to others should mean that you have worked through potential pros and cons, and have identified appropriate solutions. Thoroughly researched, analyzed and detailed concepts always make the later work stages easier.

Detail design stage

In an architectural contract, this work phase would relate to the final proposals and the production of the final drawings and specifications that will form the contract for construction companies.

Construction stage

Once the contractor is appointed, the designer's role tends to become reactive, as he or she responds to questions from the contractor and resolves any issues they may have in sourcing the equipment specified. The designer should expect to spend some time finding solutions to construction and installation problems that were not anticipated at the design stage.

Even on a small project, the designer should allow for at least one site visit near the end of the contractor's work to identify any errors, omissions or other problems. These are usually described as snagging, and any issues that come up should be reported in writing to all parties. The contractor will then have some time to remedy the problems before finally being released from their contract. It is not unusual for the client to be told everything on the snagging list has been fixed when this is not the case. The designer should allow for a final visit to check remedial works, as it can be difficult to get a contractor back on site once they have left.

Final focus and programming

The final stage, the focus and programming session, should take place before the electrical contractor leaves the site. Timing is critical here as, obviously, all the lighting must first be installed and fully operational. In addition, installation problems (such as wrongly wired circuits) do not become apparent until the control system is programmed. The lighting designer is the only person who has a complete understanding of what the lighting system should do, and a project cannot be considered complete until he or she has overseen the final positioning of any adjustable luminaires and the setting of levels on the control system.

This stage should not be seen as an addition to the design process. In lighting design, the final adjustments are critical to the creative process. Most lighting designers consider the final focus and concept stages the most creative parts of a lighting project.

Client handover

The final task is for the designer to hand the completed project over to the client and ensure they have all the information they require to operate and maintain the lighting scheme correctly. This often involves including drawings that have been updated to record any changes during construction or site works. It is also useful to provide drawings that allow the client to see what lamps are used in each luminaire type so that sourcing the correct replacements will be easier. This revised information set is usually called the as-built package, and should be a record of what was actually built and installed rather than what was planned in the design phase. The as-built package is often included in the contractor's responsibilities, but it is still worthwhile for designers to update their own drawings to reflect the reality of the final installation.

Case study St Machar's Cathedral, Aberdeen, UK

Lighting design Malcolm Innes Design

St Machar's Cathedral is a typical example of an ancient religious building that has been destroyed and rebuilt several times. It is built on a sixth-century Celtic religious site, and the current structure is built around two fourteenth-century sandstone towers; later additions and remodelling have left an eclectic mix of architectural styles and details. The austerity of the interior, with raw sandstone walls and flagstone floor, is offset by a magnificent timber ceiling that spans the nave. Constructed in 1520, the ceiling is richly decorated with 48 heraldic shields of the kings of Europe, the pope, archbishops of Scotland and the king of Scotland and his nobles. It is unique and the cathedral attracts high numbers of tourists every year.

An outline lighting brief was given to the lighting designer by LDN Architects, the project architects. This was followed by a meeting on site to look at the building, examine the existing lighting installation and discuss the client's requirements. The client liked the lit effect of the existing scheme, installed around 20 years previously, but thought there could be an energy saving by upgrading the lighting equipment. The designer had researched the cathedral before the site visit, and knew the congregation aspired to be an eco-congregation and to reduce its carbon footprint. The existing lighting scheme used tungsten and tungsten halogen lamps throughout. This provided a very good quality of light, but with high running costs and short lamp life. Existing pendants used screw-in 500-watt tungsten lamps with an average life of 1,000–2,000 hours. Relamping was done from

the ground by volunteers who used a specialist telescopic pole. The building was not suitable for using a scaffold tower without dismantling and rebuilding it to reach every pendant position. An industrial scissor lift had been used previously, but the weight had cracked the sandstone paving of the historic building.

Analysis of needs

It was clear that a significant saving in the running costs could be made. However, tungsten light sources provide excellent colour rendering and the client had already noted that they liked the quality of the existing light. Furthermore, given the nature of the building and some of the light-sensitive objects to be illuminated, it would be vital to maintain the quality of light. Therefore, only the highest-quality light sources could be used to reduce energy without losing quality.

The existing scheme did not feel overly dim and the client was not too concerned about light levels, but the light was not concentrated in the places it was needed most. The designer was keen to improve the functional light level for the congregation and ensure better illumination of the spaces the cathedral's many visitors wanted to see. This would require a general increase in light levels and had to be achieved within the parameters of reducing total energy usage.

Options using metal halide or fluorescent light sources were examined to weigh up the capital cost against the savings in energy and maintenance. It became clear that light levels

could be increased, quality maintained and architectural features highlighted, and it would still be possible to achieve a 65 per cent reduction in running and maintenance costs.

Initial concept

For this project, the general concept for the lighting design was set out in the feasibility report. It included providing ambient lighting from pendant luminaires mounted in the aisles, uplighting the timber soffit over the nave from clerestory level, and enhancing the lighting of the choir area for concerts and performances with theatrical spotlights mounted in concealed locations at clerestory level. Spotlights would pick out important artefacts and details at ground level.

A meeting was held on site with the client group (in this case, the minister and committee members responsible for the physical upkeep of the cathedral). This was not a client group who were used to meeting with design teams. Therefore, rather than produce a slick PowerPoint presentation to be shown around a meeting-room table, an informal, walking meeting was held in the cathedral so that the issues with the existing lighting could be seen clearly. Paper handouts were produced to show the committee what the proposed lighting scheme would look like. This approach worked well for the group, as they had a chance to comment and add important insights into the way the existing lighting was operated. They felt they had a chance to influence the proposals rather than simply being presented with a fait accompli.

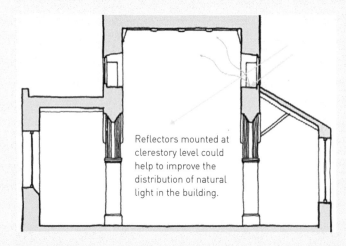

Reflectors mounted at clerestory level could help to improve the distribution of natural light in the building.

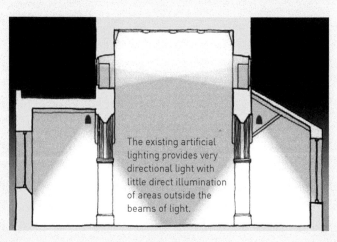

The existing artificial lighting provides very directional light with little direct illumination of areas outside the beams of light.

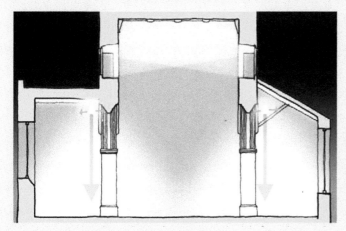

One option could be to reuse the existing positions with a light fitting that provides some uplight to the soffits of the aisles.

Typical detail of existing clerestory level showing exposed heating pipes running full length of the building with floodlights attached to the pipes. The existing lighting can be seen from ground level.

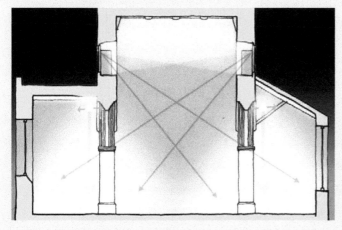

Potential lighting positions at clerestory level would be much less visible from ground level while providing additional light for central pews and for highlighting features within the aisles.

A simple mesh walkway would provide much safer access to the lighting and protect the heating pipes. Low-profile fluorescent uplights would be positioned so that they are invisible from ground level.

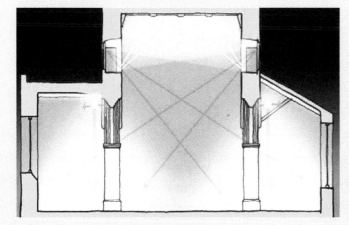

General uplighting to the heraldic ceiling can be supplemented with narrow spotlights to pick out the individual shields.

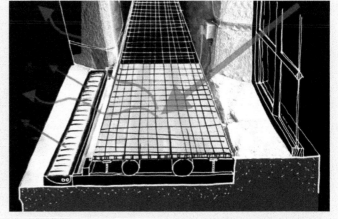

The addition of a reflector at the window recesses would enable better distribution of natural light over the heraldic ceiling. The reflector could be as simple as a section of treadplate.

Opposite
Sketches illustrating conclusions drawn from the initial analysis study.

Above
Sketch analyses of proposed and existing lighting for the lighting feasibility study.

Opposite
View of the cathedral looking towards the altar. Linear fluorescent uplights are mounted on the ledges of the clerestory openings to illuminate the carved and painted heraldic ceiling over the nave.

Top right
False-colour render created using DIALux lighting calculation software. This view of the north aisle shows the pendant luminaires mounted at 7.1 m above floor level. The result is a very bright spot of light directly above the luminaire and little light on the underside of the arch.

Top far right
In this calculation, the pendant luminaires have been lowered to 6.4 m above the floor level. The uplight on the soffit above is much more even and the underside of the arches is illuminated.

Bottom right
Key for false-colour renders of the north aisle. Illumination levels are in lux (lumens per square metre) and represent the light falling on to the surfaces.

Bottom far right
False-colour render showing a general view of the cathedral. In this image, each luminaire position is marked by the yellow wireframe cage. This symbolizes the pattern and direction of light produced by the luminaire (the photometrics). The uplights mounted at clerestory level are illuminating the timber soffit over the nave.

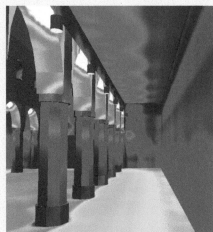

Illuminance contours in lux

200	
175	
150	
125	
100	
75	
50	
25	
0	

Scheme design

Although luminaire layout ideas were explored in sketch form on paper, an important part of the project had to rely on computer-based tools that would normally be used at a later part of the process. Because the designer wanted to maintain as many of the existing wiring locations as possible to reduce costs and potential damage to the historic fabric, calculation software was used at an early stage to test the effect of different luminaire options. It was also important to ensure that the uplit effect on the various soffit surfaces would not be visibly uneven. This could only be achieved through a careful balance between the optics of the uplights and the distance between them and the surfaces they were to illuminate. The clerestory uplights were a fixed distance away from the timber soffit, so the quality of the

optics became paramount in the selection of these luminaires. The uplight for the aisle soffits was planned to derive from pendant positions, which meant the pendant height would affect the pattern of illumination. If the uplight was too close to the soffit there would simply be a very bright area close to the luminaire and little spread of light beyond. A lower-mounted luminaire would provide a more even spread of light. However, this was opposed to the aesthetic desire to position the pendants high up to reduce visual intrusion into the historic setting of the cathedral. The calculation software allowed a compromise position to be found and tested virtually.

The modelling of the light from the clerestory and aisle pendants allowed the designer to prove that the same light sources could provide light for the congregation and illuminate the

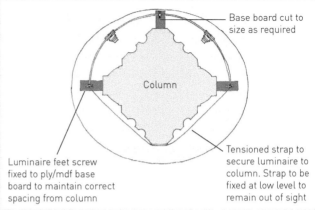

Base board cut to size as required

Column

Luminaire feet screw fixed to ply/mdf base board to maintain correct spacing from column

Tensioned strap to secure luminaire to column. Strap to be fixed at low level to remain out of sight

Left and above
Photograph and detail plan showing how the custom ring of spotlights is mounted on the column head without any mechanical fixings into the stonework. A thin, tensioned wire strap runs around the column to hold the luminaire securely in position. Each luminaire holds up to six spotlight heads. Each head is adjustable and lockable so that the precise focus is retained during any future maintenance. The luminaire sits on softwood timber blocks to provide correct spacing and prevent contact between the height-adjustable metal legs and the stonework. The final, simplified solution for securing the column-head spotlights reduced costs by eliminating additional components that would have needed to be specially made.

architectural structure of the space, without the addition of new wiring positions. With this issue resolved, concentration turned to providing some additional feature lighting to improve the visual experience for cathedral visitors.

The aisles contained a number of architectural features and ecclesiastical artefacts such as the sculptural stone font, a carved wooden triptych wall panel and a series of stone funerary effigies. These elements had previously been illuminated by the ambient light of the overhead lighting. This did not provide a good quality or direction of light, especially as wall-mounted objects were viewed against the side windows, which made it difficult to see the artefacts during daylight hours. A specific layer of lighting was included in the design to highlight these artefacts, and architectural details – spotlights were wired on separate circuits from the pendant lighting to allow independent switching, and were intended principally for use when there were visitors in the cathedral.

Various options were explored to determine the best locations for the spotlights to the aisle artefacts. It was initially hoped that they could be mounted in concealed locations at clerestory level. However, a close examination of all the areas to be lit and the potential viewing angle of each clerestory window showed that not all areas could be lit from these locations. The eventual solution was to work from the column heads with very discreet spotlights. Some of the columns had previously had a now-redundant lighting position, so wiring already existed in many locations. This wiring was tested and reused where possible. The designer investigated many options to find a suitable spotlight that would be physically small and adjustable to cover objects at ground level or on the walls. It was decided that wherever possible, mechanical fixings would be avoided to prevent damage to the historic stonework. It also became apparent that no existing spotlight luminaires would do the job without significant compromises. The solution was to create a custom luminaire.

The custom-designed luminaire consisted of a semicircular alloy ring, curved to fit the column and containing multiple spotlight heads. Each spotlight was individually adjustable and lockable and contained a glare shield to reduce distracting glare when viewed from ground level. They were designed around a low-voltage tungsten halogen dichroic reflector lamp. The design of the custom luminaire was a close collaboration between the lighting designer and the lighting manufacturer.

Considering that the rest of the scheme uses very efficient light sources such as linear fluorescent and metal halide, it may seem odd to use a low-voltage tungsten halogen lamp for the spotlights. However, the particular lamps selected proved to be the best choice when all other options were examined. Very high-quality, energy-saving low-voltage tungsten halogen lamps were selected, as they provided the best combination of quality of light, low cost, small physical size, efficiency (the infrared energy-saving lamps specified use around 30 per cent less energy

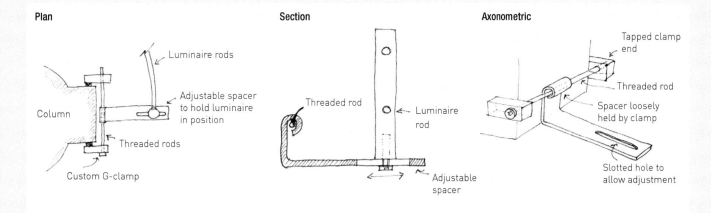

Plan

Luminaire rods

Adjustable spacer to hold luminaire in position

Column

Threaded rods

Custom G-clamp

Section

Threaded rod

Luminaire rod

Adjustable spacer

Axonometric

Tapped clamp end

Threaded rod

Spacer loosely held by clamp

Slotted hole to allow adjustment

Above
Various options were explored to allow the column-head spotlight luminaires to be attached securely without having to drill the stonework. Design by sketching is an important part of the scheme design stage.

Below
Detail design drawing for the custom column-head luminaire (below left). This was issued to the manufacturer to show design intent. The final shop drawings were produced by the manufacturer, and checked and approved by the designer before manufacture.

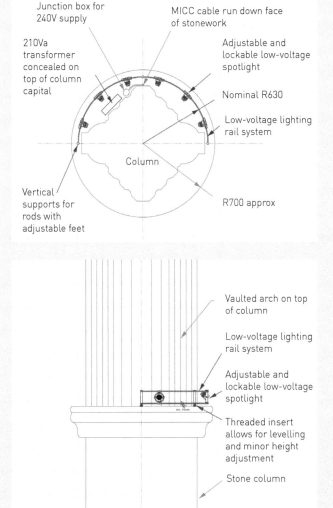

Junction box for 240V supply

MICC cable run down face of stonework

210Va transformer concealed on top of column capital

Adjustable and lockable low-voltage spotlight

Nominal R630

Low-voltage lighting rail system

Column

Vertical supports for rods with adjustable feet

R700 approx

Vaulted arch on top of column

Low-voltage lighting rail system

Adjustable and lockable low-voltage spotlight

Threaded insert allows for levelling and minor height adjustment

Stone column

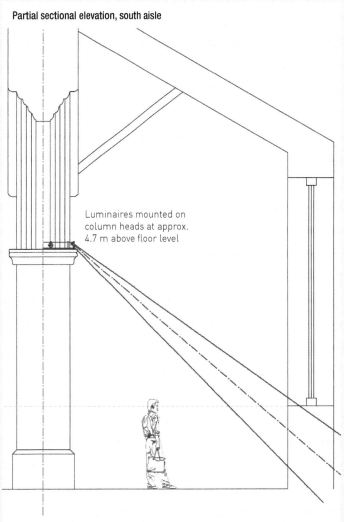

Partial sectional elevation, south aisle

Luminaires mounted on column heads at approx. 4.7 m above floor level

than a traditional dichroic lamp) and lamp life (the average lamp life of 5,000 hours will be extended by very slight dimming and is likely to be closer to 10,000 hours).

Throughout the project, careful consideration was given to the future maintainability of the lighting installation, as there is little point in installing a well-considered, aesthetically pleasing lighting scheme that will fail because it is not possible to reach the luminaires for relamping and repair. Long-life lamps were used in the least accessible locations, such as the clerestory uplights and the pendants in the aisles. The proposed replacement luminaires used metal halide lamps with an average life of 12,000 hours, but lamps could not be changed using a pole, as

had been the case with the existing fittings, and the difficulties involved in using various types of access equipment are discussed earlier. The solution was to mount the pendants on electric winches, which would allow them to be lowered to ground level for maintenance. This added to the capital cost of the project, but would be offset by not requiring hire of access equipment and two days of an electrician's time.

Lighting control options were discussed with the client at this stage. In bright daylight, the pendants can be switched off and natural light can provide all the ambient lighting for the space. The uplights to the heraldic ceiling and the spotlights to the aisle artefacts can be switched on when there are visitors in the building, and the

pendant lights can be switched on for services or when natural light levels are low, such as on winter afternoons. Much of the switching of circuits could have been automated using a lighting control system with daylight sensing, and this was originally proposed. However, as the building was always staffed, the clients wanted to retain manual control of the lighting rather than rely on a pre-programmed control system that may be difficult for untrained volunteers to use.

Opposite
The new pendant luminaires direct most of their light downwards to illuminate the pews and aisles. However, the inclusion of a translucent section in the upper part of the reflector allows a proportion of light to escape upwards to illuminate the ornate plasterwork of the soffit. The height of the pendants was also set to allow the uplight to catch the upper part of the stone arches. Column-mounted spotlights are used to highlight the wall hanging, the stone font and the cross mounted on the far column.

Above left
The mounting height for the pendant luminaire was selected to provide uplight to the soffit and the top of the stone archway without intruding too much into the line of sight through the arches. A remotely controlled electric winch is housed in the cream-coloured boss above the pendant. The winch is used to lower the luminaire to ground level for maintenance.

Above right
The original scheme. The pendant downlights provided no upward lighting component, leaving the timber soffit of the aisles very dark. The lack of any directional lighting, and strong daylight coming in through the large, south-facing stained-glass windows, made viewing the wall-mounted artefacts very difficult.

Above

Column-mounted narrow-beam spotlights subtly pick out wall- and floor-mounted artefacts from their background.

Left

The redesigned scheme includes spotlighting to pick out the artefacts and memorials so that they are clearly visible to the cathedral's many visitors. This does not require a lot of light – just enough to lift the artefact out from the background ambient illumination provided by the new pendant luminaires.

control channel	luminaire reference	location	description	quantity	lamp type	lamp load	circuit load	control type
1	AE	chapel	suspended pendant with integral electronic control gear for 150 W metal halide lamp. To be supplied with etched glass reflector/diffuser and clear glass safety cover	2	metal halide	150 W	300 W	switch
2	AE	aisles	suspended pendant with integral electronic control gear for 150 W metal halide lamp. To be supplied with etched glass reflector/diffuser and clear glass safety cover	11	metal halide	150 W	1,650 W	switch
3	AG	balcony	wall-mounted luminaire with low-glare asymmetrical optics and integral control gear for linear T5 fluorescent lamp. Luminaire to be used to downlight balcony floor level	2	metal halide	54 W	108 W	
4	AH2	chapel	adjustable and lockable low-voltage MR16 spotlight heads with backspill protection for above. To be used only with IRC type MR16 lamps, max 35 W	8	low-voltage	35 W	280 W	tungsten dim
5	AH2	aisles	adjustable and lockable low-voltage MR16 spotlight heads with backspill protection for above. To be used only with IRC type MR16 lamps, max 35 W	38	low-voltage	35 W	1,330 W	tungsten dim
6	AA	clerestory plus 2xAF on balcony	asymmetrical uplight for 54 W T5 linear fluorescent lamp. To be supplied with integral dimmable control gear	18	fluorescent	54 W	972 W	
7	AC	clerestory (focus to table)	track-mounted spotlight to illuminate choir and pulpit below	2	tungsten	375 W	750 W	tungsten dim
8	AC	clerestory (focus to choir)	track-mounted spotlight to illuminate choir and pulpit below	6	tungsten	375 W	2,250 W	tungsten dim
9	AC	clerestory (focus to Bach Choir)	track-mounted spotlight to illuminate choir and pulpit below	2	tungsten	375 W	750 W	tungsten dim
10	AL	choir stalls	allowance for repair or refurbishment of existing candle branches	2	LED	8 W	17 W	
11		shop	allowance for lighting to shop				1,200 W	switch
12		vestibule	allowance for lighting to vestibule				1,200 W	switch
13		external	allowance for external lighting				1,200 W	switch

Above
Lighting control schedule for the project. The control channel number relates to the layout drawings and identifies which luminaires should be switched or dimmed together.

9. Recording and visualizing lighting

Words rarely manage to capture our experience of light effectively. It is important to find a visual language that will help to record and explain light and lighting effects to others. There are many techniques that create visual imagery, some of which claim varying degrees of realism, but a 'realistic' image often fails to express the essence of a lit environment as well as a simple sketch.

As designers, we need to identify the method and medium appropriate to the task of describing our ideas. Every technique has its place, but it is a good principle always to use the simplest one that conveys what we want to say. Complex techniques may require lots of time, and can introduce unimportant details that get in the way of the lighting story.

Below
This quick tonal sketch is not intended to be an accurate representation of the architecture, but the student who drew it has managed to capture the lit effect of the space. The drawing has a clear sense of the directional quality of natural light flooding in through large windows.

Drawing and sketching

With the ease of access to so many digital methods of creating imagery, it is easy to overlook the quickest and, often, the most effective ways of recording lighting ideas. Drawing and sketching require the simplest of materials and can be used as a form of analysis to help understand and record the mechanics of a space or the pattern of light within an existing space. Drawing can also be used to capture a feeling or mood – we have an incredible ability to respond emotionally to tones on a sheet of paper. Drawings are, by their very nature, a great way of editing out unimportant information so that we can concentrate on the principal features of a scene. Thumbnail sketches are often the clearest possible way of communicating an idea to others; there are no distracting details and no extraneous information to divert attention from the message you want to convey. The power and flexibility of drawing and sketching should not be underestimated.

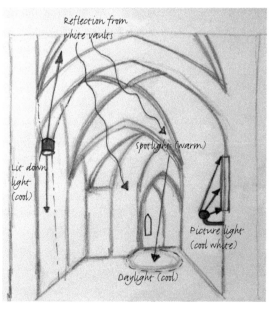

Left and above
In analyzing an existing space within a cathedral, a student made a tonal drawing that captures the pattern of light and shade (left), and a diagrammatic sketch that identifies the locations of luminaires and the direction of the light they produce (above).

Abstract representation

While abstract representations are rarely a good way of explaining ideas to other people, they can sometimes be invaluable in describing the more technical aspects of lighting. Despite the great sophistication of three-dimensional rendering software, the resulting images are no substitute for the experience of standing in the real illuminated space. One of the greatest drawbacks of most image formats, both printed images and, especially, display screens, is that they have a very narrow dynamic range compared to the human visual system. Even a high-quality computer display is likely to have a brightness range 1,000 times smaller than the human eye can typically perceive.

A number of different software packages allow the designer to produce accurate lighting calculations using real photometric data for the lamps and luminaires being proposed. These packages should not be confused with three-dimensional modelling and rendering software, which rarely uses real-life luminaire data. In the few instances where the software can use real photometric data, the output is still directed towards creating a realistic image rather than producing useful technical information for the professional. Unlike high-end three-dimensional modelling software, some of the most widely used professional-quality packages (such as DIALux and Relux) are free to the user; the cost is borne by the lighting manufacturers, who provide the real-world luminaire data used in the calculations. However, free does not mean the packages are easy to use. Professional lighting calculation software has a steep learning curve and can only be mastered once the user understands the basics of manual lighting calculations. Nevertheless, it allows a skilled user to test design ideas quickly in a virtual environment and fine-tune designs before equipment is installed.

Professional lighting calculation software allows us to understand the subtleties of how the designed lighting may perform in a space. However, it is clear that simply producing a photographic-style render will tell us very

Below left
False-colour render showing a general view of a cathedral. Each luminaire position is marked by a yellow wireframe cage. This symbolizes the pattern and direction of light produced by the luminaire (the photometrics). The uplights mounted at clerestory level illuminate the timber soffit over the nave.

Below right
False-colour render from DIALux lighting calculation software. This view of the south aisle of a cathedral shows the pendant luminaires mounted at 6.4 m above floor level. The uplight on the sloping soffit does not look very even, but the 50–150 lux range is not overly contrasty. It would take a 10:1 difference to be significant.

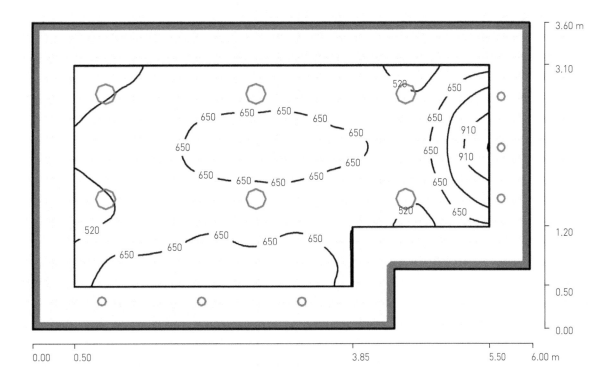

0.00   0.50   3.85   5.50   6.00 m

little about the real visual experience of the lit space, so one option is to use an abstract representation of the light that is either received or reflected by surfaces.

False-colour images are used extensively in scientific imagery to present information, such as temperature, population density and election results that cannot be seen by the naked eye, and which is made visible with coloured overlays on maps. False-colour renders can be produced by calculation software to depict areas of equal illuminance.

It is important to remember that these images are a designer's tool; it is rarely desirable to include them in presentations, as false-colour renders are easy to misread. The colours are often deliberately lurid to emphasize the steps between levels and their relative visual brightness may have no relation to the actual light levels they represent.

Above
Another way of presenting lighting calculation results is with an isolux contour plan. An isobar weather map shows areas of equal atmospheric pressure, while a geographical contour map shows areas with equal elevation above sea level. An isolux plan shows areas of equal illuminance. The central shape on this drawing connects parts of the calculation surface that are illuminated to 650 lux, while the closely spaced lines on the right-hand wall demonstrate a steep increase in light levels here, rising above 910 lux. Note that an isolux plan such as this will typically show the illumination at desk height, not on the floor surface.

Diagrammatic representation

Almost all architectural drawings are diagrammatic. That is, they show a simplified and schematic representation of structures rather than presenting any kind of realistic image. Architectural, engineering and other technical drawings have a language of line types and line weights that needs to be understood before the viewer is able to fully decipher the drawing. When producing information for people outside the design profession, you need to watch your language. In the same way that you cannot expect clients to understand all the technical jargon and phrases that accompany lighting, you should not expect them to be able to easily understand the implied meaning of technical drawings.

Although non-specialists may have trouble with the subtle details of an architectural plan, almost everyone has a highly developed understanding of diagrammatic visual language. Tapping into this common language can help to convey complex information easily.

One of the most potent symbols that can be used to explain light is the arrow. The path of light may be invisible to us, but the direction from which it hits a surface makes a significant impact upon the lit effect of any space. A single arrow in a lighting diagram can imply both the location of a light source and the intended focus for that light. People tend to intuitively understand the size of an arrow as having some relationship to quantity – a large arrow from a light source suggests more light than a small arrow from another source. Colour quality can be suggested, with daylight arrows being a different colour from electric light ones.

There are many more diagrammatic methods that can be used to help people understand lighting proposals. Examples of photo collage can be seen on page 131, where photographs of the existing site have been overlaid with drawn elements to demonstrate design ideas. In the illustrations on pages 160 and 161, rendered section drawings are collaged onto a sunset background to add interest and time of day context. Sometimes the effectiveness of simple photographic manipulation cannot be beaten, as shown in the sequence on pages 94 and 95.

Whatever the illustrative technique chosen to help people understand lighting proposals, the most important information to deliver is usually the location of the luminaires and what areas or surfaces they will illuminate. Once that is understood, other information can be included. Always try to ensure that each presentation image is as succinct as possible; too much information can make drawings unreadable. If you were trying to describe the scene in words, you would split the description into paragraphs to aid legibility; you should do the same with drawings, using separate images to tell different parts of the story.

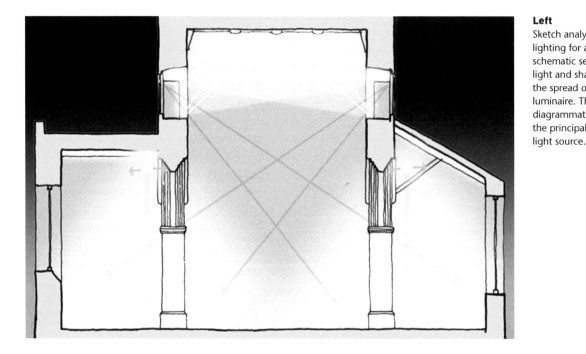

Left
Sketch analysis of proposed lighting for a cathedral. The schematic section drawing uses light and shade to indicate the spread of light from each luminaire. The drawing also uses diagrammatic arrows to indicate the principal direction for each light source.

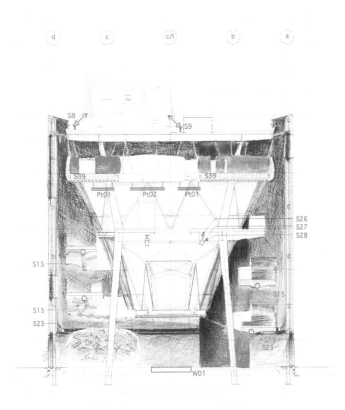

Left

This presentation drawing by Kevan Shaw Lighting Design shows a section through the circulation space of a multipurpose arts venue, the Public, West Bromwich, UK. Built on a CAD drawing, it shows the location of luminaires in red and adds a hand-drawn render of the vibrant colour of the internal space. This kind of image allows all the members of a design team to understand the location of the lighting and the lit effect it will produce.

Below

Also built on a CAD drawing, this section of the same project has been rendered in Photoshop to produce a more polished result. This kind of image is typically used for a PowerPoint presentation to the client. The actual locations of the luminaires are not important in this case, so they have been omitted and only the lit effect is shown.

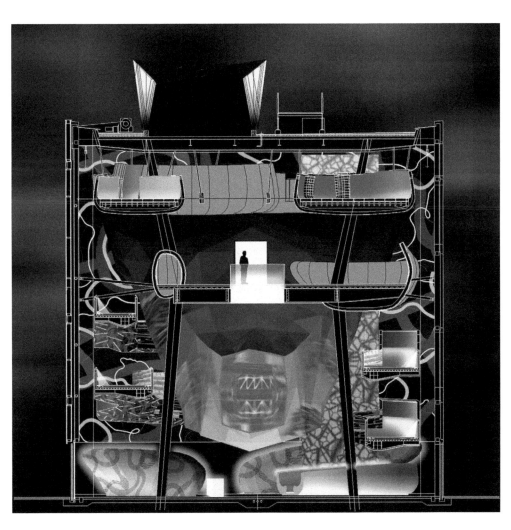

Photography

When it comes to recording scenes the way we experience them, the phrase 'the camera never lies' has probably never been true. While there are passing similarities between a camera and our eyes, the processing and recording mechanisms are so radically different that photography can never hope to record exactly what we see. Part of the problem is that what we 'see' is only partly to do with the visual information gathered by our eyes, and has a lot to do with the brain adding layers of interpretation and past experience to try to make sense of the visual data.

Photography can be very useful for recording what a scene looks like, but this is not the same as recording what it feels like. All forms of photography are restricted by having a much lower dynamic range than the visual system. The higher contrast of film and digital photography makes for a simplified view that is, literally, more black and white than our visual experience of the

same scene. Techniques such as high dynamic range (HDR) photography, where several different exposures are combined into one image, attempt to match our vision more closely. But the further restrictions presented by the limited dynamic and colour ranges of printing and screen-based image display mean designers should be aware that photography is not the same as seeing.

If photography is our only record of a site we have visited, we have probably not looked at the space properly. Even the two minutes it takes to produce a simple thumbnail sketch provides an infinitely better appreciation of the three-dimensional geometry, structure and pattern of light in a space. As a recording medium, photography works best as a way of reminding the designer what he or she actually experienced. Nevertheless, as long as its limitations are recognized, photography can be useful for recording lighting tests and mock-ups in order to show the design ideas to others.

Opposite and left
Photography can be useful for recording lighting tests and demonstrating the benefits and pitfalls of a lighting solution. These before (opposite) and after (left) images show how the dark, cave-like quality of a reception area was transformed by the addition of fluorescent uplighting mounted on top of the canopy, making the scene much more of a visual attractor. However, the images also reveal the problem created by the gloss paint on the soffit, which creates a specular reflection that allows the fluorescent luminaires to be seen reflected in the ceiling (the white patches on the ceiling). The camera has exaggerated the contrast in the scene, and this has overemphasized the reflection problem. However, this can help to make the problem clear to others and demonstrates that any permanent lighting solution would have to work around it.

Computer renders as a design tool

When the structure that is to be illuminated does not yet exist at design stage, computer models can be useful tools to assist the design process. The capability of computer rendering systems to produce images that look photographic has to be recognized as a real distraction during the design phases of a project. This process is about using the render as a tool for the designer, not creating a presentation image for the client. A good computer model may have no more realism than a simple card model and yet it can still be invaluable to the lighting designer. If a set of real questions can be defined as the purpose for creating the model, then valuable time can be saved. The designer only needs to include just enough detail and accuracy in the model as is required to answer the questions, speeding up the modelling process. A model can help to answer various questions, such as: what areas can be illuminated from certain locations; will shadows be cast by structural elements; will luminaires be visible from ground level, and will mounting systems allow enough adjustment to perfect the focus on site? These questions can be difficult to resolve in complex three-dimensional environments such as the roof truss in the illustrations below. Three-dimensional computer models can often help designers where simple sections and elevations cannot.

Right
This model for the Great Hall of Stirling Castle was produced and illuminated in 3ds Max. The historic building was being completely reroofed, so site tests were not possible. The CAD model did not use the real photometric measurements of the proposed luminaire, but did allow placement of accurately sized luminaire models on the wall head, to investigate general beam-spread requirements, any potential shadowing by structural elements and the concealment of the luminaires when viewed from ground level.

Below right
This image of the completed installation for the Great Hall shows that the lit effect is a very close match to the computer renders created at design stage by the lighting designers Speirs and Major Associates. A series of 150 W ceramic metal halide (CDM) spotlights are positioned on the wall head between the roof trusses and they light across the roof to illuminate the structure on the opposite side. Additional 70 W CDM spotlights located at the wall head are focused downwards to illuminate the opposite wall. This means all the ambient light at low level is reflected from the wall and roof surfaces and the luminaires do not create a glare problem for visitors who look up at the roof structure. Although the exact photometry for each luminaire type was not available for the CAD model, the designers' experience allowed them to produce a render they knew would resemble the final lit effect closely enough to be a valuable visualization tool.

Left
Two images produced from a computer model built and rendered in DIALux. The images show two lighting scenes for a boardroom with bright ambient light from recessed fluorescent luminaires (top) or narrow-beam spotlights directed on to the table (bottom). For white light projects, renders without colour allow the viewer to concentrate on the lit effect rather than the oddities of any texture maps used in the model.

Physical models

It is now easy and relatively quick to create good-quality computer models, but designers still use physical models to test and record design options. The limited range of brightness levels available on a computer monitor means that, although computer modelling has a particular role in the design process, physical models can tell us things about light that computer ones cannot.

Physical modelling also allows designers to get a live, hands-on feel for how small changes can influence the lit effect. On simple models, materials can be changed very quickly to test ideas as they occur. No matter how complex the inter-reflection of light off many surfaces, with physical models the results are instant and there is no waiting for models to render.

Below
Even simple card models can be useful for testing lighting ideas. Here students are exploring ideas to control and redirect sunlight in a south-facing room. To prevent direct sunlight entry, the optimum angle of the louvres depends on the height of the sun in the sky and will therefore change throughout the year.

Above left

Simple models may not provide a high degree of measurable accuracy, but they are invaluable for testing ideas and determining what is worth investigating more fully. Even experienced lighting designers sometimes resort to crude card models and torches to test or demonstrate the basic principles of a lighting idea.

Above right and right

The hands-on nature of a physical model allows for quick and easy experimentation. Discarded materials such as reflective food wrappers (above) can be pressed into service to test the lit effect a polished light shelf would have compared to that created by a matt white reflector (right).

Above and opposite
Physical models also play an important role in large-scale projects. This example is a section of Terminal 4, Madrid Barajas Airport, designed by architects Richard Rogers Partnership with Estudio Lamela. The photographs were taken by the lighting designers Speirs and Major Associates, who took the model outdoors to see how the solar shading would work with the low-angle afternoon sunlight.

Below
This lighting plan for a restaurant is
annotated to explain the different
luminaires required, and also
includes manufacturer's details and
specification for installation.

10. Project communication and completion

Lighting schemes are not constructed from rendered images, but CAD drawings rarely describe all that is required of a lighting installation. A lighting drawing sometimes has to be a hybrid of objective technical detail and esoteric artistic direction. During the production of a detail design package, the lighting designer must constantly ask: what information is needed to ensure the lighting scheme is delivered just the way I envisaged it?

Recessed downlight
Manufacturer:
Modular Lighting
Instruments

Recessed downlight
Manufacturer:
Modular Lighting
Instruments

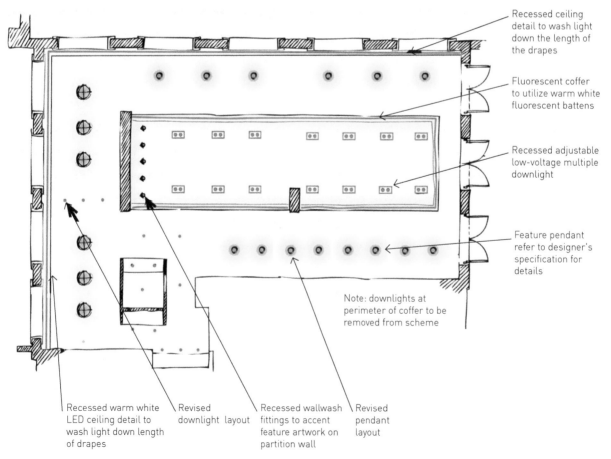

Recessed ceiling
detail to wash light
down the length of
the drapes

Fluorescent coffer
to utilize warm white
fluorescent battens

Recessed adjustable
low-voltage multiple
downlight

Feature pendant
refer to designer's
specification for
details

Note: downlights at
perimeter of coffer to be
removed from scheme

Recessed warm white
LED ceiling detail to
wash light down length
of drapes

Revised
downlight layout

Recessed wallwash
fittings to accent
feature artwork on
partition wall

Revised
pendant
layout

What is enough information?

When preparing lighting design drawings and specifications, it is important to ensure that you provide enough information for someone who knows nothing about the design proposals to nevertheless understand your intentions. The design process tends to be confined to the design team and client body, yet designers rely upon contractors who know nothing about that process to deliver their designs.

To make your drawings understandable, try to see them through the eyes of the people who will be using them. Drawings produced on CAD can suffer from many problems when they are printed – for example, line weights can collapse to very light weights. Drawing luminaire symbols at scale can be useful to ensure equipment will fit into the available space, but when printed to scale the symbols can become almost invisible. It is much better to be bold with them, to ensure they are obvious. A good lighting layout drawing combines accurate scale drawing and schematics.

Architectural drawing sets tend to be based on floor plans, but lighting is often mounted on the ceiling. Often, it is necessary to create ceiling plans in order to ensure

that the proposed lighting layout will work around any high-level obstructions.

Lighting layout drawings should include enough dimension information to locate each luminaire accurately. It should also be easy to identify the luminaire types, either by creating different symbols or by adding a letter or number code to each luminaire position. It is a good idea to identify control groups on the layout drawings.

There are occasions when plan views cannot provide all the necessary information about how or where luminaires should be installed. In such a case, a section or elevation drawing will help the contractor to visualize how the lighting is to be arranged or where it should be directed. Detail drawings are also invaluable to ensure important features are not missed – even a hand-drawn sketch can communicate the kind of positioning information that it is difficult to convey in words. A lighting information package is all about communication. You should make use of any combination of measured drawings, sketches and schematics that you think will make it easy for someone else to understand your ideas and intention.

Below
Annotated sketch drawing for the same restaurant as opposite.

Section drawings are particularly important in buildings with varying ceiling heights. The section allows the contractor to understand exactly where each type of luminaire is to be located. This section is created as a schematic drawing because it is intended to show all the luminaire types even though no straight section would cut through all the luminaire positions. The drawing is described as a schematic because it is not based on any architectural base drawing or survey. The lighting designer has created a rough section based on site measurements. The diagrammatic nature of the drawing allows the designer to add arrows to indicate the aiming direction for each luminaire and the approximate spread of light from spotlights and pendants.

Sections and elevation drawings

Plans are useful for layouts that are on one horizontal plane, but it is difficult to indicate vertical positioning on a plan. Elevation drawings are often the only way to describe how lighting is arranged in a space or where it is to be focused. Section drawings can also be invaluable for this task, but careful consideration should be given to where the cuts are taken. It may be best to consider section drawings as being more schematic than true sections as this will allow luminaires to be shown even if they are concealed by a structure.

A schematic section can be invaluable in enabling the contractor installing the lighting to understand why it needs to be positioned in the locations indicated. It is not unknown for a contractor on site to report that a proposed lighting location is not going to work because a ventilation duct has been installed between the luminaire and the surface to be illuminated. It is difficult to convey the lighting design intent with only plan layouts.

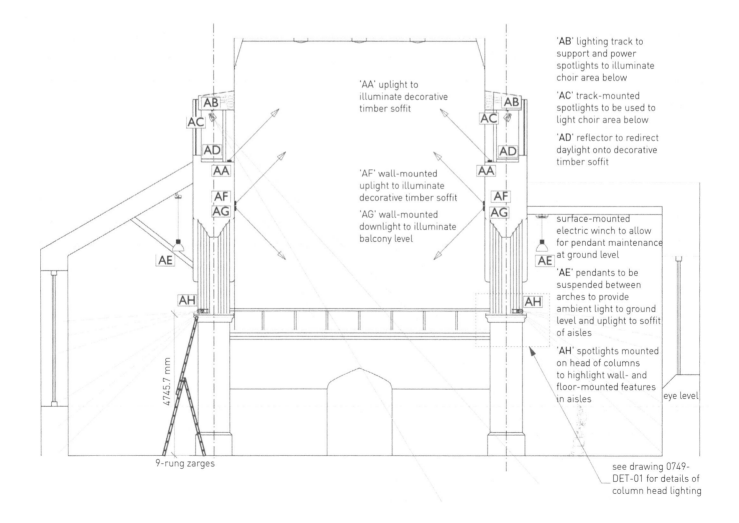

'AB' lighting track to support and power spotlights to illuminate choir area below

'AC' track-mounted spotlights to be used to light choir area below

'AD' reflector to redirect daylight onto decorative timber soffit

'AA' uplight to illuminate decorative timber soffit

'AF' wall-mounted uplight to illuminate decorative timber soffit

'AG' wall-mounted downlight to illuminate balcony level

surface-mounted electric winch to allow for pendant maintenance at ground level

'AE' pendants to be suspended between arches to provide ambient light to ground level and uplight to soffit of aisles

'AH' spotlights mounted on head of columns to highlight wall- and floor-mounted features in aisles

eye level

4745.7 mm

9-rung zarges

see drawing 0749-DET-01 for details of column head lighting

Left and below
Crystals at City Center, Las Vegas, architecture by Studio Daniel Libeskind, lighting design by Focus Lighting. With complex geometry such as the façade of this building (left), the clearest way to explain the lighting design is with a series of sections and elevations. The drawing by Focus Lighting (below) includes details of each lighting element and a long section to show their location within the site. The drawing uses subtle colour tints to communicate the purpose and focus for each luminaire position.

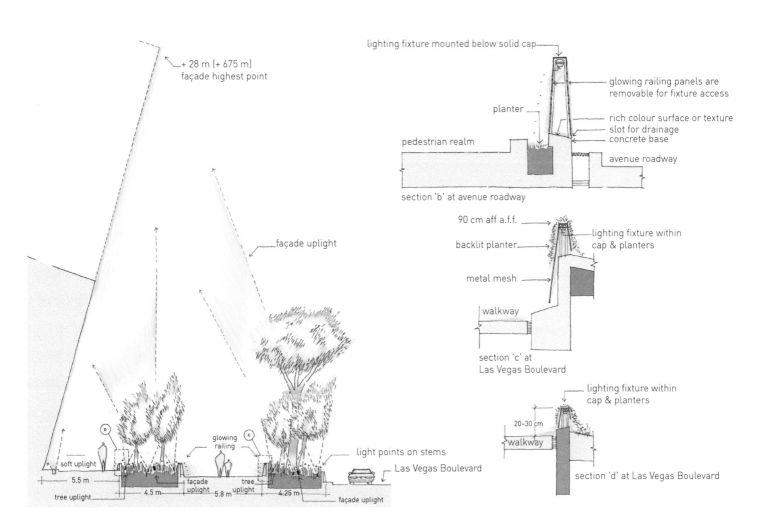

Case study Musée de l'Orangerie, Paris, France

Lighting design Anne Bureau Concepteur Lumière

Architect Brochet Lajus Pueyo

Sitting on the edge of the Tuileries gardens, next to the Seine river in central Paris, the museum occupies an elaborate former greenhouse built in 1852 to house tropical fruit. The building was reworked in 1927 to contain two elliptical galleries designed specifically to display Claude Monet's masterworks *Les Nymphéas* (*The Waterlilies*). The latest major conversion project was completed in 2006 and created a series of underground galleries to display a collection of Impressionist paintings. The existing elliptical upper galleries were retained, but the lighting system was radically redesigned and improved. The new system brought the gallery up to twenty-first-century conservation standards without radically altering the look of the 1920s interior.

Right

The original 1927 gallery had a simple gauze screen between the artworks and the glass roof of the orangery. This would have done little to prevent the paintings being exposed to high daylight levels, which could have been potentially very damaging. The new scheme introduces a conical 'lamp shade' over each gallery to control the amount of daylight that enters. The daylight is reflected by the matt white surfaces of the lamp shade to provide indirect illumination and is then softened by a thin gauze screen positioned to replicate the original design. This provides a diffuse light that still retains a sense of connection to the outside world.

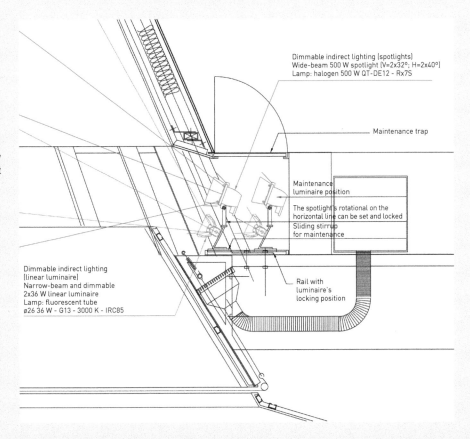

Lighting of the lamp shade
Narrow-beam linear luminaire 2 x 36 W
Fluorescent tube ø26 36 W - G13 - 3000 K - IRC85

Dimmable indirect lighting (spotlights)
Wide-beam 500 W spotlight (V=2x32°; H=2x40°)
Lamp: halogen 500 W QT-DE12 - Rx7S

Dimmable indirect lighting (linear luminaire)
Narrow-beam and gradable 2x36 W linear
luminaire
Lamp: fluorescent tube ø26 36 W - G13 -
3000 K - IRC85

Above and right

The lighting designer created a sophisticated artificial lighting system that mimics the pattern of natural light within the space. The overall section (above) and section detail (right) show a ring of luminaires concealed in a lighting slot above the gauze screen. There are two banks of luminaires: narrow-beam fluorescent battens and wide-beam tungsten floodlights. The luminaires are positioned to light across the void and illuminate the inner face of the lamp shade. Both sets of luminaires are dimmable and are controlled with a daylight tracking system, which gradually increases the electric light to maintain a relatively constant illumination level in the gallery.

Dimmable indirect lighting (spotlights)
Wide-beam 500 W spotlight (V=2x32°; H=2x40°)
Lamp: halogen 500 W QT-DE12 - Rx7S

Maintenance trap

Maintenance
luminaire position

The spotlight's rotational on the
horizontal line can be set and locked

Sliding stirrup
for maintenance

Dimmable indirect lighting
(linear luminaire)
Narrow-beam and dimmable
2x36 W linear luminaire
Lamp: fluorescent tube
ø26 36 W - G13 - 3000 K - IRC85

Rail with
luminaire's
locking position

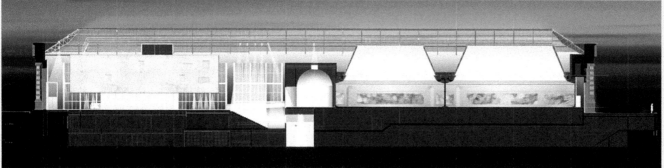

Top

The underground corridor gallery is toplit with heavily filtered daylight. The lowered soffit above the painting prevents too much direct light hitting the display wall on the left. Instead, the wall is illuminated with ceiling-recessed, dimmable fluorescent wall-wash luminaires. At night, the natural light is replaced with uplight luminaires positioned above the concrete beams.

Above

The project is best understood in section. Here a long section ably describes the ground floor of the building. The entrance is to the left and runs under the elevated sandstone insertion. A bridge takes visitors over the void to the lower floor and into the two linked Monet galleries on the right of the image. The section shows the height of the lamp shade daylight controls above the galleries.

Above
The lower galleries are predominantly lit with a ceiling-recessed fluorescent wall-wash system. The warm white 3,000 K fluorescent lamps are colour-matched to the low-voltage tungsten halogen spotlights that are track-mounted to provide a subtle accent light where required.

Left
Schematic short section through the museum showing the entrance bridge on the right that takes visitors into the two ground-floor Monet galleries. Moving down the stairs, visitors come to the daylit basement corridor gallery. The main gallery rooms on the left are entirely artificially illuminated.

Lighting renders

The term 'render' tends to make us think of computer renders, but architectural renders existed long before there were computers to produce them. To render an image simply means to depict it artistically – by hand, by computer or by any combination of the two. Three-dimensional computer modelling and rendering have largely supplanted the role of the architectural illustrator, yet it is widely recognized that even the most sophisticated rendering software produces images that lack an esoteric quality found within renders produced by hand. It is ironic that the current trend in modelling software is to produce rendering engines that can replicate the inaccuracy and smudgy quality of hand-drawing. There is a place for photorealism in architectural renders, but humans often seem to be much more comfortable with the imperfect results of drawings made by hand.

As any professional lighting designer will tell you, even the most physically accurate and fastidiously calculated and rendered architectural scene cannot replicate the feeling of being in the space. One of the most severe limitations of computer rendering systems is the method of output. A typical computer monitor may have a brightness scale (contrast ratio) of around 1,000:1. This sounds impressive, but it represents only one-thousandth of the range over which the human visual system can operate. The result is that when we are in a real lit environment we can see a huge amount more detail in

Left
Computer renders have real limitations and cannot produce the same visual effect as actually standing in the space. It is therefore often better to deliberately eschew any attempt at photorealism when you are producing a lighting render. If the information can be conveyed effectively with a hand-drawn render, that is likely to be the fastest way to produce the required image. Of course, the accuracy of a hand-drawn render depends on the lighting experience of the designer and his or her skill with a pencil. This image of the natural and artificial lighting within an imaginary space was produced by an interior architecture student. This kind of hand-drawn render is within the capability of anyone who takes the time to examine how light interacts with architectural space. Even if your drawing skills are not up to presentation standards, the discipline of producing hand renders will make it much easier for you to identify mistakes and perceptual inaccuracies in computer renders.

the bright areas and shadows than a computer monitor or printout can ever replicate.

This is not to say that computer renders are not useful tools for the lighting designer. Clients tend to believe renders produced by computer and often see them as some kind of sample of reality. This can be good – and bad. For a computer render to produce useful lighting results it must not only utilize measured photometric data from the actual luminaires used in the project; the model must also include the correct colours, textures, patterns and materials for every surface in the scene. Given that renders are usually produced at relatively early stages of a project, it is highly unlikely that all the materials finishes will have been determined. The computer modeller often has to guess what some of the materials, colours or furniture will be, which means that the lit effect can never be considered completely realistic.

The level of photorealistic detail computer renders can produce frequently causes other problems when lighting renders are presented to clients. The presentation about lighting can quickly be diverted by discussions about the particular texture of leather displayed on the seating or the pattern of marble used on the walls. Architects and designers therefore need to be very careful in their use of computer renders; sometimes it is prudent to dispense with some realism in order to focus discussions on the task at hand.

Below
This render was produced in 3ds Max, an Autodesk-owned three-dimensional modelling program that includes the ability to use real luminaire photometry to produce more accurate results. It was a presentation image to demonstrate the lit effect of a design for a conference room. An experienced designer is able to determine how accurate a computer render is, and is able to adjust image brightness or contrast to better match how users will actually perceive a space. This render, done as part of the design process, is a very close match to the completed project.

STEP BY STEP USING COMPUTER MODELS

This set of images was produced by New York lighting designers OVI. Even though the model appears to be cardboard, it was actually produced in AGi32, a professional lighting calculation and modelling software program. The model was deliberately created without colour and the shapes of the figures were given the appearance of two-dimensional cut-outs to concentrate attention on the lit effect. In the same way that a sketch section drawing does not show the final construction detail, it is clear that these images are not intended to show

exactly how the project will look when completed. Yet the lighting here is photometrically accurate. The software uses measured data of real luminaires to calculate the lit effect. This is far superior to the very crude lighting effects produced by 90 per cent of three-dimensional design software. Specialist lighting calculation software such as AGi32 does not have 'spotlights' and 'floodlights' as in most three-dimensional software – it only uses real luminaire data.

1 In this model and the one below, the designers experimented with supposedly similar luminaires from different manufacturers to gauge the difference in the lit effect. Here they try mounting a row of downlights near the vertical surface and lighting the benches from underneath.

2 In this version, the row of downlights is mounted over the benches as opposed to close to the vertical surface.

3 In this model and the one below, the different components of the scheme are isolated. Here the model shows what the space would look like if it were lit only by uplighters, and how the addition of light below the benches helps to create a subtle but important visual lift in this area.

4 This version shows how downlights prevent people being silhouetted against the lit wall.

Recording circuiting and control intent

A diagrammatic layout that clearly indicates how luminaires are to be grouped for control or switching purposes is invaluable in ensuring that the scheme is installed the way that you intend. It is helpful to include circuiting and layout information on one drawing. Where this is not possible, the control drawing can be created as a very bold, schematic layout so that it is not confused with the dimensioned layout plan.

Even where CAD drawings exist, there are advantages in preparing a set of circuiting or control drawings on paper. A red pen mark-up of layout drawings is a fast and simple way of ensuring that you have broken the scheme down into logical control areas and that similar areas are grouped correctly. This drawing can also help to identify where user controls should sensibly be located. It is very difficult to get this global view of a project when zoomed into the detail of an on-screen CAD drawing – you should check printed versions of drawings frequently to maintain this overview.

Right
This drawing for a hotel bedroom shows luminaire positions in red, along with dotted lines for control circuits and numbered wall switches for each circuit. The hand-drawn layout, done at scheme design stage, is deliberately sketchy but shows the lighting much more clearly than is usually possible in CAD. This kind of drawing can also be used more easily in PowerPoint presentations to keep the client informed of progress. Once the principle of the control arrangement is agreed with the design team, a CAD drawing can be produced for inclusion in a detail design package.

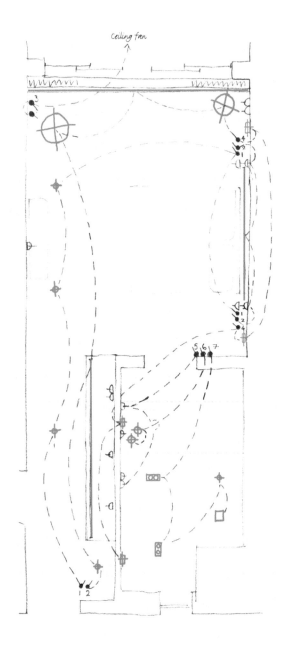

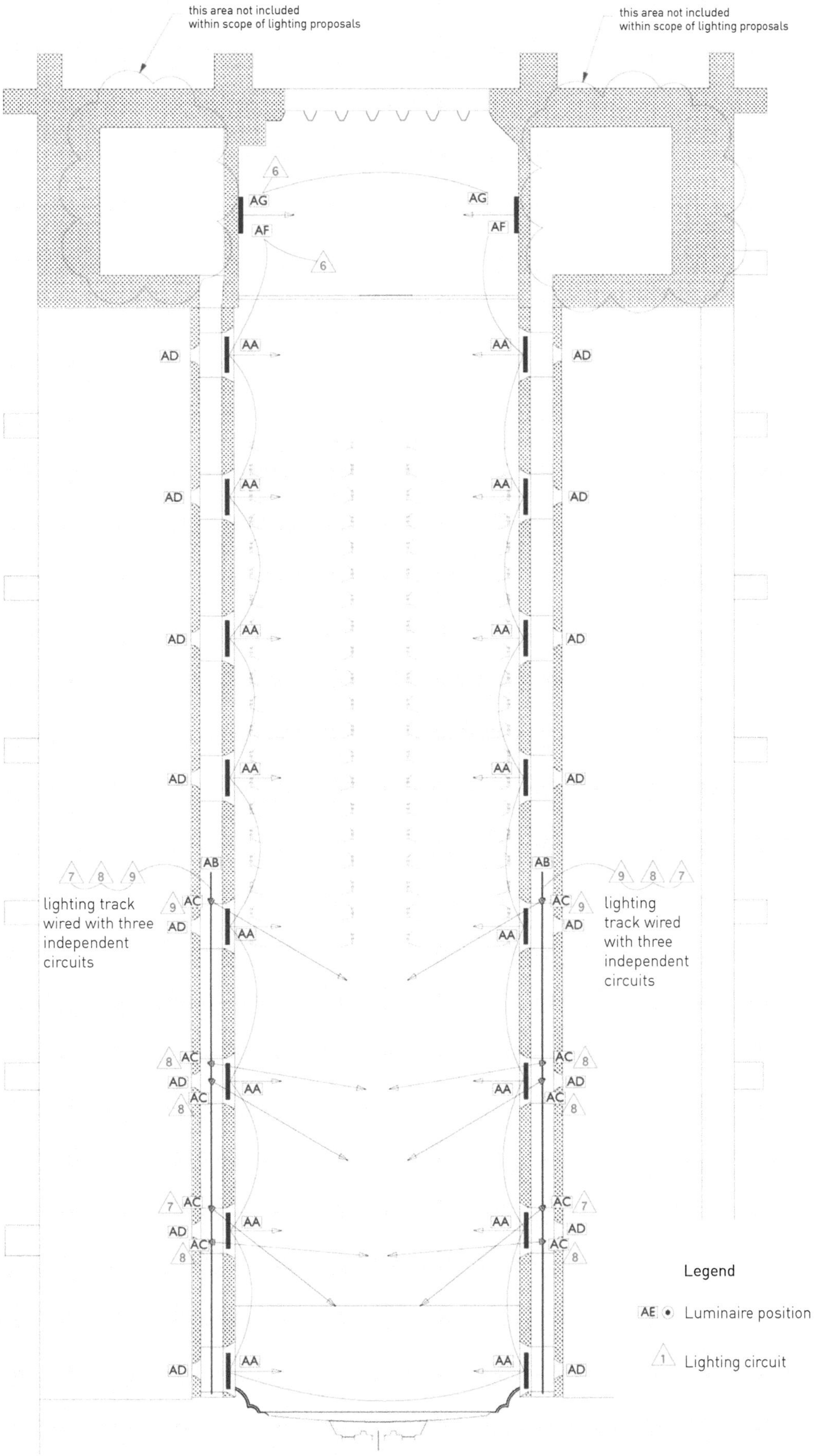

this area not included
within scope of lighting proposals

this area not included
within scope of lighting proposals

AG
AF

AG
AF

AD   AA
AD   AA
AD   AA
AD   AA

AD

AD

AD

AD

AB

AB

7   8   9

lighting track
wired with three
independent
circuits

9   AC
AD   AA

AC   9
AD   AA

9   8   7

lighting
track wired
with three
independent
circuits

8   AC
AD
AC
8

AA

AA

AC   8
AD
AC
8

7   AC
AD
AC
8

AA

AA

AC   7
AD
AC
8

AD   AA

AA   AD

Left

Lighting diagram of the clerestory level of a cathedral. Lighting layout drawings should convey specific information about the design. While it is sometimes useful to draw luminaires to scale, it is more important for them to be obvious on the drawing. In this diagram, lighting elements are shown in blue and the architectural base drawing is greyed out. Each luminaire position is given a clear two-letter reference code, which is repeated on the technical specification document. The drawing also indicates the control circuiting as red lines that connect all the luminaires that will be switched or dimmed together. The numbers in red triangles refer to control circuit numbers listed in the separate control schedule document. Control circuits shown do not necessarily indicate the actual wiring to be installed, as control groups are often broken down into separate wired circuits to make installation easier or prevent overloading of the wiring.

Legend

AE • Luminaire position

△ Lighting circuit

Use of sketch details

Sketches are far more important in the design process than
many people imagine. CAD drawings produce defined
lines and are capable of high levels of accuracy. This
implies that they are always accurate, drawn to scale and
can be measured from. However, the lighting designer
often needs to communicate design intent without
knowing all the precise measurements or specifications of
other materials.

With a sketch, the designer has control over exactly
what is shown and what is left out. A sketch detail can be
used to deliver only the information that is relevant to the
lighting installation without the drawing becoming a mess
of extraneous detail.

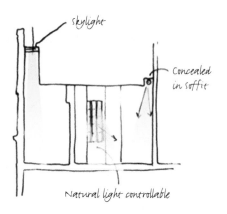

Concealed soffit lighting, skylight and
controllable daylight/view at window

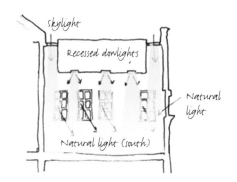

Natural southern light through windows
and skylight, artificial recessed downlights

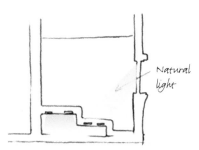

Recessed lighting beneath built-in
furniture, to create private zones

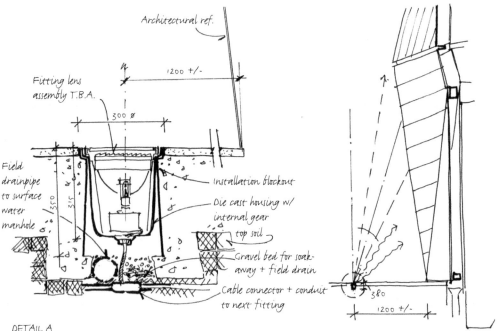

DETAIL A
GROUND BURIAL UPLIGHT (EXTERIOR - TYPICAL)

EVENT SPACE - EXTERIOR SECTION /ELEV

Below

An effective lighting presentation can be produced without the use of time-consuming computer renders and Photoshop manipulations. Sometimes a pencil, a few words and some supporting images are all that is required to tell the whole story of a lighting proposal. This student project provides a lot of information on one easily read board. Photographs of the existing building are on the left, with the imagined reworking of the architecture shown as a sensitive hand-drawn tonal render on the right of the board. A set of simple hand-drawn sections describes the architectural proposition and the use of natural and artificial light within the main atrium space. This is supported by a set of thumbnail sketches that show the principle for the various lighting solutions. The package is rounded off with a summary of the design intent, and supporting images of similar lit effects from other projects.

Host building (south-facing)

Main staircase & stained glass window

Typical warm wood

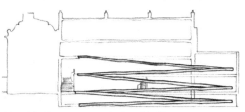

Memorialization space – ramps rise through building

Natural light through stained glass & interplay on ramps

Concealed artificial light (warm) to enhance wood and aid journey along ramps

Tonal study of memorialization space

Concealed, diffused lighting underside of ramps

Concealed lighting in ramp handrail

Concealed, diffused soffit lighting along corridor

Design intent

- Existing polished wood is luminous and reflective, giving depth and richness
- Psychologically evokes sense of warmth, reliability and support
- Emphasize this with warm artificial light to pick up orange/yellow undertones
- Mood should be hospitable and peaceful, enabling visitors to use space as they wish
- Green will complement warm wood and represents reassurance, balance and peace
- Replace existing windows with stained glass – colours to be stronger as building rises
- Diffused colour will change depending on time of day and season
- Maintain connection with exterior, without glare or views to tenements opposite
- Ramp undersides have concealed, diffused artificial lighting, to highlight walkway below

Lighting mock-ups and tests

There are many reasons to create physical tests of lighting proposals. It may be surprising that experienced lighting designers rely heavily on tests and mock-ups, but it is experience that has taught them to appreciate the benefits of physical testing. An observant designer knows the limitations of drawings and computer models, and how they can never totally replicate the experience of being in a lit space.

Physical models can be used at all stages of a project to test or demonstrate ideas. Remarkably simple scale models (see illustrations on pages 150–1) can demonstrate the complexity of shading and inter-reflection visible in the world around us. Large-scale mock-ups can help to convince clients that the lit result is worth the effort. Full-size mock-ups can allow the whole design team to understand the tolerances required to make the lighting scheme work (see the case study of Morimoto Restaurant, on page 122). The design team can then work together to ensure that the lighting equipment can be positioned in just the right location.

Physical tests and full-scale mock-ups are invaluable tools for the lighting designer and are used on projects from the smallest retail units through to the largest airports (see pages 152–3). Professional designers know that there is no substitute for a real-life lighting test.

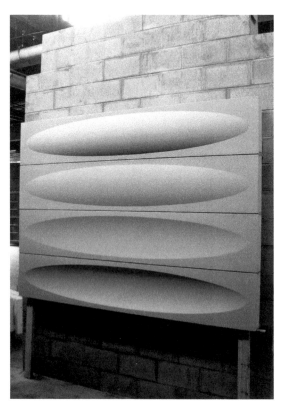

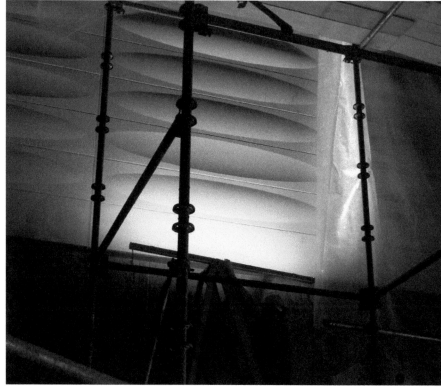

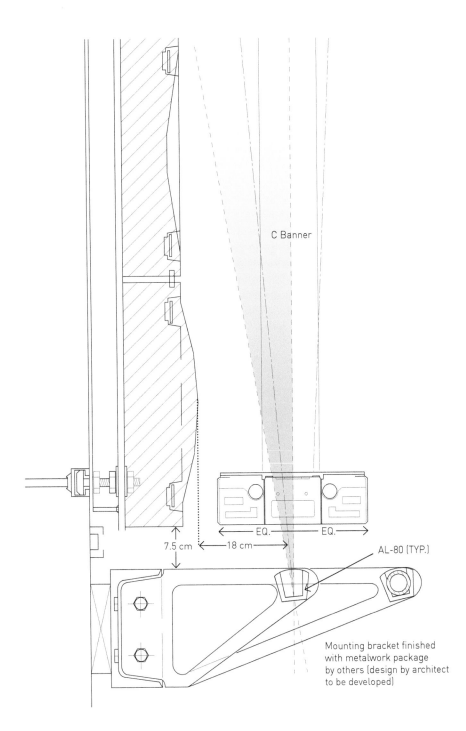

C Banner

EQ.   EQ.

7.5 cm   18 cm

AL-80 (TYP.)

Mounting bracket finished
with metalwork package
by others (design by architect
to be developed)

Left
This is the final installation detail
for the project opposite. This
detail and the dimensions were
established with the help of a
full-scale mock-up. The lighting
designers also used full-scale
mock-ups to determine the finish
to the wooden wall panels in order
to avoid reflected glare.

TIP FULL-SCALE MOCK-UPS

Large-scale tests should not be seen as
a sign of indecision or lack of knowledge
on the part of designers. Instead, it is the
extent of their experience that tells them
when a test is vital to perfect a lighting
solution. An experienced designer knows
the limitations of modelling techniques
and how important a physical test can
be. If it is possible to test a design, you
should. At the very least, you will be able
to demonstrate to others the lit effect you
intend. It is also possible that the test will
identify potential problems before it is too
late to make any changes.

Specification documents

Lighting projects can unravel because of poor or incomplete specification documents. Taking a methodical approach to itemizing exactly what is required will pay dividends by ensuring you get exactly the equipment and effects that you asked for. It is worth remembering that, along with construction drawings and details, specification documents form part of the legal contract that defines what the contractors should supply and build. Because these are legal documents, it is wise to be meticulous about them to ensure they cannot be accidentally or intentionally misread. No matter how small or rushed the project may be, it is helpful to produce two stages of documentation: generic and detailed specifications.

Generic specification

This represents the information required for an outline specification as would be issued at scheme design stage. The final choice of luminaires has not been made, but you should be able to define the following general features of each luminaire type.

- What is it? (e.g. an adjustable downlight, an exterior floodlight, a colour-change spotlight...)

- Where is it? (e.g. recessed into the ceiling, mounted on a window ledge, attached to a lighting track...)

- What is it for? (e.g. directed towards the wall to highlight paintings, uplight to canopy, feature spotlight to display of bar glasses...)

- What type of light source is it? (e.g. low-voltage tungsten halogen, dimmable cool white fluorescent, RGB colour-mixing LED...)

A good generic specification document will succinctly describe all there is to know about your design intent, short of naming the actual manufacturer and part number. As such, it will form the basis of the detailed specification.

Detailed specification

The final specification document at detail design stage should build upon the generic specification. It requires methodical thinking to hone the description of each luminaire in order to ensure there can be no confusion about what it is for, where it is to be positioned, and all the parts and accessories needed to make it work. Manufacturer's catalogue information is invaluable, but it is worth getting the manufacturer to check the part numbers of the luminaires and accessories before the specification is issued and becomes a legal tender or bid document.

In many countries, it is common to specify a single manufacturer for each luminaire type. By contrast, in the US, specification documents usually have to name more than one manufacturer for each item. Even in countries where this is not normal practice, such as the UK, it can still be required for large projects. As there is no such thing as identical luminaires from different manufacturers, multiname specifications make it difficult for the designer to ensure the best results. The International Association of Lighting Designers (IALD) produces a very useful document entitled 'Guidelines for Specification Integrity', which helps designers with this difficult task.

Opposite
An extract from a final specification document for a landscape lighting project. The two-letter references are noted adjacent to each luminaire on the drawings. There is a detailed description of the type of luminaire, where it is to be located and any accessories required. The manufacturer and part number information allow the contractor to order the correct parts. It is sometimes not permitted to specify a single supplier and the designer has to write a detailed 'performance specification' for each luminaire, to ensure the equipment supplied will do what is required of it. Just because luminaires look the same rarely means they will perform the same.

ref	description	manufacturer	part number	accessories	quantity	lamp	lamp load	total load
LA	Exterior rated cast aluminium ground-recessed uplight. Luminaire to have machined stainless steel top plate. Luminaire to be mounted flush with the paving and set into carved recess in feature wall/stone bollards. Supplied with stainless steel recessing sleeve. To be powered from remote transformer.	Louis Poulsen	5747760006	anti-vandal screws 5747760116	52	Osram – Decostar IRC 35 W 24°	35.0 W	1,820 W
	Exterior rated 20-50VA 12V transformer for ref. LA uplight. Transformer to be mounted in recessing chamber below luminaire, one transformer per luminaire.	to be sourced by contractor			52			
LB	Exterior rated ground-recessed LED uplight in IP67 stainless steel housing with bonded acrylic rod. Luminaire to be set into recess in feature wall/ bollards to function as a marker light. To be powered from remote transformer.	AC/DC Lighting	Spek – ACDC1031/ WW/SSN/ (MI-special-LB)	500 mm long, 45 mmø frosted acrylic rod, bonded to luminaire front glass	54	integral Luxeon 1 W Warm White LED	2.4 W	130 W
	Exterior rated IP65 24V DC remote electronic transformer for ref LB. To be mounted in concealed location. 8 ref. LB luminaires per transformer. Luminaires to be wired in star pattern with max cable length of 100 m between transformer and luminaire.	AC/DC Lighting	ACDC1903		7			
LC	Exterior rated ground-recessed linear marker light using ultra long life LED light source. Luminaire to be mounted flush with the paving to minimize visual intrusion. Luminaires to be nominal 2 m long and utilize warm white LEDs on 18 mm centres. To be powered from remote transformer.	AC/DC Lighting	Linton – ACDC1006/ WW/2000/18/ rear cable entry	ground-recessing channel to be sourced by contractor. Refer to drawing 0520-SK-03 for details.	24	integral warm white 5 mm LEDs	17.2 W	413 W
	Exterior rated IP65 24V DC remote electronic transformer for ref LC. To be mounted in concealed location. Maximum 4 m linear length of ref. LC luminaires per transformer. Luminaires to be wired in star pattern with a maximum cable length of 20 m between transformer and luminaire.	AC/DC Lighting	ACDC1903		12			
LF	Exterior rated IP67 ground-recessed very narrow-beam uplight with tilt lockable and adjustable beam optics and integral control gear for 150 W metal halide lamp. Luminaire body to be cast aluminium, top plate to be stainless steel. To be ordered with ground-recessing housing. Luminaire to be used to illuminate column of monument.	iGuzzini	B025 Light Up Walk Pro	BOOS recessing sleeve	12	Philips Master Colour CDM-T 150 W/830 G12	150.0 W	1,800 W
LG	Exterior rated IP68 ground-recessed uplight with wall-wash optics and integral electonic control gear for 35 W CDM-T lamp. Luminaire body to be cast aluminium, top plate to be stainless steel. To be ordered with ground-recessing housing. Luminaire to be used to illuminate base of monument.	Erco	33715.000 Tesis	33962.000 cast aluminium recessing housing	12	Philips Master Colour CDM-T 35 W/830 G12	35.0 W	420 W

Realizing the project

Contractors are sometimes seen as the enemy of the design team, but they can make or break a project and it is always worth taking the time to talk to them as equals. They have a difficult job, and if you respect their problems everyone will get on much better. A contractor who understands and respects what you want to achieve, and why you want to achieve it, always produces a better project. One of the most critical times is the end of the construction phase, when there is a rush towards completion. This is when good relations with contractors can pay dividends.

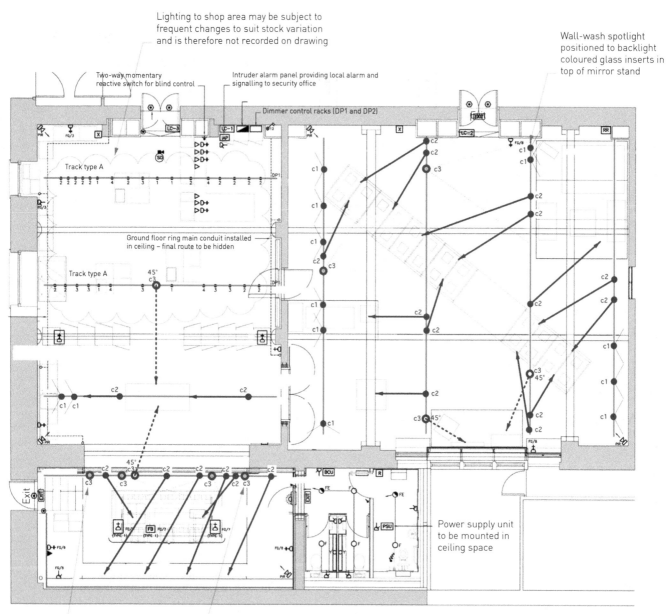

Lighting to shop area may be subject to frequent changes to suit stock variation and is therefore not recorded on drawing

Wall-wash spotlight positioned to backlight coloured glass inserts in top of mirror stand

Two-way momentary reactive switch for blind control

Intruder alarm panel providing local alarm and signalling to security office

Dimmer control racks (DP1 and DP2)

Track type A

Ground floor ring main conduit installed in ceiling – final route to be hidden

Track type A

Power supply unit to be mounted in ceiling space

Spotlight focused down to highlight timber truss

Spotlight focused down to highlight timber truss

Final focusing and programming

A project is never complete until it has been focused and/or programmed by the designer. The hands-on aspect of site work is a vital learning tool to help him or her to improve future projects and avoid repeating any mistakes. In the hurry to complete late-running projects, it is easy for contractors to see the final focusing stage as unwarranted additional work, but the designer must insist it is done properly. Without someone on site who knows exactly what was intended with the design, and precisely where each luminaire should be focused, the project may never be as good as it should be.

Below and opposite

In any project with adjustable lighting, it is likely that a lot of adjustments will be made on site, which means the original layout or focus drawings will become out of date. If there is to be any chance of keeping the design intent through future maintenance, it is important to record the as-built information. This drawing shows the as-built lighting for a gallery. All the luminaires are track-mounted, so, for each luminaire, the drawing records its type, its physical location, its aiming direction and the track circuit to which it is connected (most lighting track has three independent circuits). As the drawing is intended for the end user and any maintenance staff, it includes illustrations of each luminaire and the replacement lamp type, making it the only document required for relamping and general maintenance.

Legend
Track circuit from which spotlight is powered
(this is not critical for the exhibition lighting)

Description: Track-mounted wall-wash spotlight used to evenly illuminate vertical surfaces from close offset.
Lamp supplied: 100 W 12V QT12 capsule
Relamp with: Philips 203561 70 MasterCapsule
60 W 12V IRC axial burner capsule

Description: Track-mounted medium spotlight
Lamp supplied: 100 W 12V 24° ARIII
Relamp with: Philips 411150 10 MasterLine III
60 W 12V 24° ARIII, IRC, UV filter reflector lamp

Description: Track-mounted medium floodlight
Lamp supplied: 100 W 12V 45° ARIII reflector lamp
Relamp with: Philips 411136 10 MasterLine III
60 W 12V 45° ARIII, IRC, UV filter reflector lamp

Description: Track-mounted narrow spotlight with spread lens
Lamp supplied: 100 W 12V QT12 capsule
Relamp with: Philips 203561 70 MasterCapsule
60 W 12V IRC axial burner capsule

Project: Furniture Gallery

Drawing title: As Built Exhibition Lighting Layout

Drawing no: 0873

Scale: not to scale

Revision: 0

Date: 2010

Below

Although programming can only be completed on site with everything in position, a lot can be achieved in advance of site work. At design stage, it is worth producing a rough idea of how many different scenes will be required and what the different dimming levels may be for each control channel. This information is valuable to help distill the control requirements and ensure the control system manufacturer can deliver what you require. Like the luminaire specification, a detailed lighting control specification would be issued as part of the contractual documentation for the project. However, the kind of pre-programming document shown here is typical of the communication that would happen between the lighting designer and control system manufacturer or programmer prior to the beginning of their work on site.

control channel	luminaire ref	location	description
1	AE	chapel	suspended pendant with integral electronic control gear for 150 W metal halide lamp. To be supplied with etched glass reflector/diffuser and clear glass safety cover
2	AE	aisles	suspended pendant with integral electronic control gear for 150 W metal halide lamp. To be supplied with etched glass reflector/diffuser and clear glass safety cover
3	AG	balcony	wall-mounted luminaire with low-glare asymmetrical optics and integral control gear for linear T5 fluorescent lamp. Luminaire to be used to downlight to balcony floor level
4	AH2	chapel	adjustable and lockable low-voltage MR16 spotlight heads with backspill protection for above. To be used only with IRC type MR16 lamps, max 35 W
5	AH2	aisles	adjustable and lockable low-voltage MR16 spotlight heads with backspill protection for above. To be used only with IRC type MR16 lamps, max 35 W
6	AA	clerestory plus 2xAF on balcony	asymmetrical uplight for 54 W T5 linear fluorescent lamp. To be supplied with integral dimmable control gear
7	AC	clerestory (focus to table)	track-mounted spotlight to illuminate choir and pulpit below
8	AC	clerestory (focus to choir)	track-mounted spotlight to illuminate choir and pulpit below
9	AC	clerestory (focus to Bach Choir)	track-mounted spotlight to illuminate choir and pulpit below
10	AL	choir stalls	allowance for repair or refurbishment of existing candle branches
11		shop	allowance for lighting to shop
12		vestibule	allowance for lighting to vestibule
13		external	allowance for external lighting

Project communication and completion **177**

scene 1	scene 2	scene 3	scene 4	scene 5	scene 6	scene 7	scene 8	scene 9	scene 10	scene 11	scene 12
daytime bright daylight	daytime av. daylight	daytime low daylight	sunset–midnight	midnight–sunrise	evening function option A	evening function option B	evening large choir	daytime service	watchnight service	spare 1	spare 2
off	on	on	off	off	off	on	off	on	–	–	–
off	on	on	off	off	off	on	off	on	–	–	–
off	off	70%	off	off	50%	100%	50%	100%	–	–	–
off	95%	80%	off	off	100%	off	100%	off	–	–	–
off	95%	80%	off	off	on	off	on	off	–	–	–
100%	80%	70%	off	off	70%	70%	70%	100%	–	–	–
off	off	off	off	off	90%	90%	90%	95%	–	–	–
off	off	off	off	off	90%	90%	90%	95%	–	–	–
off	off	off	off	off	off	off	90%	off	–	–	–
off	off	off	off	off	80%	100%	100%	100%	–	–	–
on	on	on	off	off	on	on	on	on	–	–	–
off	on	on	on	off	on	on	on	on	–	–	–
off	off	off	on	off	on	on	on	on	–	–	–

Conclusion: the future

To try to predict the near or distant future for lighting design would be folly, as technologies can change very quickly. But there are some clear trends that will define the direction that lighting is likely to take. Interestingly, it is not simply the existence of new technology that is driving change, but the economic and ecological pressure to reduce energy consumption. Around the world, governments are tightening energy efficiency targets for lighting installations and instigating outright bans on the sale of products that are seen as 'inefficient'. This goes beyond the well-known 'ban the bulb' programmes that will remove incandescent lamps from supermarket shelves; low-voltage tungsten halogen lamps will also be legislated out of existence for consumers and non-electronic control gear will be phased out in some regions. The steady tightening of minimum efficiency standards even means that some existing compact fluorescent lamps will fail to meet the proposed minimum standards in some regions.

What makes these tightening standards feasible is that, after a hundred years of incremental improvements in lamp technologies, we are entering a new era of lighting performance improvements. A rapid pace of improvements is more common in the computing world, where Moore's law describes the tendency for computing power to double every two years, leading to an exponential growth. It may be no coincidence that it is semiconductor technologies that have transformed the field of architectural light sources. Beginning as something of an interesting novelty, LED light sources have improved at a rate previously unseen in the lighting world. The traditional high-performing light sources such as linear fluorescent and high-intensity discharge have been improved gradually to show a three-fold increase in efficacy over a period of 70 years of development. LED light sources for general lighting took only around ten years to show a four-fold increase in efficacy. Organic Light Emitting Diodes (OLED) are still a new technology, but as solid-state lighting

Individually addressable lighting may be the future of lighting, but it has been technically feasible for many years. The advent of reliable, low-cost solid-state lighting such as LED sources has also made this level of control financially achievable for many projects. Although the American artist Leo Villareal created his *Multiverse* LED light sculpture for Washington's National Gallery of Art in 2008, it points to a future direction for many lighting installations. Multiple, low-luminance sources that can be controlled to produce movement, pattern, images or text allow lighting installations to communicate with and interact with users in a much more direct and less subtle fashion. Gradually, this kind of installation will move from being largely the preserve of well-funded art projects to an everyday device in the architectural lighting designer's toolkit. However, good design is timeless. Skilled designers will always be wary of the novelty of new techniques and will strive to use lighting technology in all forms to create or enhance lighting environments that are based on an appreciation of how light and colour affects human beings.

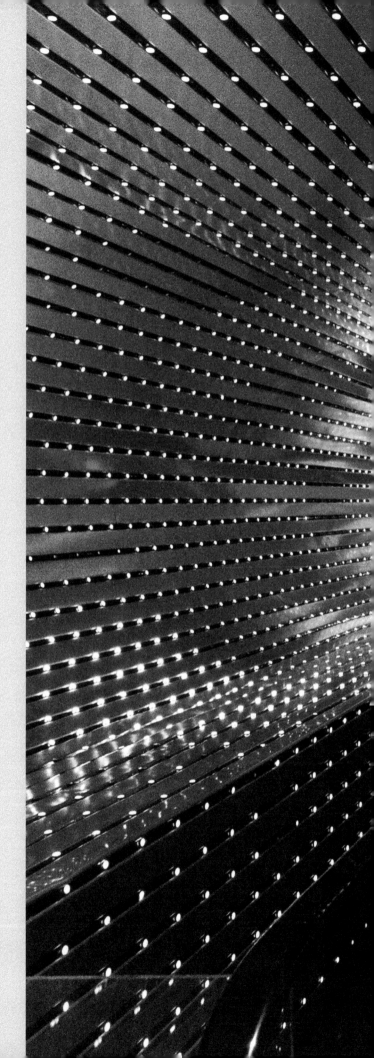

devices, it is likely that they will eventually follow a similar path of exponential increase in efficacy.

For many end users in the future, what may be more striking will be the ability to control individual light sources without complex and expensive wiring. Light sources already exist that incorporate computer networking chips to allow for live control and reporting over IP networks. Maintenance times can be improved as each luminaire or lamp is able to report a fault or failure as it occurs. This has important implications for commercial installations such as large office spaces, hotels or street lighting, where maintenance has typically been difficult or time-consuming. However, this technology will have applications in domestic spaces, where the increasingly networked home will be able to directly control individual luminaires around the house or grounds.

But this book has not focused on lighting technologies, because lighting design is much more than a sum of the technologies. Although lighting technology sometimes assists great design, it does not drive it. It was not high technology that created the seemingly impossibly tall wall wash in the main prayer hall of the Sheikh Zayed bin Sultan Al-Nahyan Mosque (page 118). It was not new or experimental equipment that produced the astonishingly beautiful luminous walls in the Morimoto Restaurant project (page 122). At One Gyle Square (page 110) it is the simplest linear fluorescent luminaires mounted in carefully designed coves that produce the dominant visual memory of the space. In each case, it was the application of relatively simple and commonplace lighting equipment with novel and well-crafted installation details that produced the captivating lit effect. It was the skill and technique of the designers, allied with their tenacity in pursuing an ambitious vision, that resulted in luminous beauty. It is hoped that this book will go some way to convince the reader that great lighting can only be created through good design practices and a deep understanding of light and its visual and psychological effect on humans. Designers who can see beyond the technology and the 'next great invention' hype of the industry and instead view the output of those technologies – the light itself – as their medium will be the kind of people who can transform our built environment into a glorious feast for the senses.

The increasing cost of energy and the desire or necessity to reduce carbon emissions will continue to drive technological improvements in lighting equipment. But it should be remembered that the most efficient lighting installation is the one that is switched off. Daylight design is key to creating a built environment that makes the best use of energy resources. This could extend beyond simply utilizing more daylight in building designs to follow the example of natural light. The range and diversity of natural light far exceeds the strict limits set for our built environments. A little more flexibility to work with darkness as well as light would allow designers to concentrate light where it is really needed. Done well, this could save power and precious materials and improve the lit effect for future generations.

Glossary

adaption
The ability of the human visual system to operate in a wide range of lighting conditions and to adapt to significant changes in the colour and intensity of light received by the eye. However, the full range of sensitivity is not available all at the same time. We can move from areas brightly illuminated by cool daylight to spaces with warm-coloured tungsten lighting and, given enough time to become adapted to the new lighting conditions, we will perceive both as acceptably well lit spaces illuminated by a white light source. (See also page 27.)

candela
The SI (*Système international*) base unit of luminous intensity. It is not a measure of absolute radiant energy from a light source, but of the radiant energy weighted by the human visual system's sensitivity to light of different wavelengths. It is a measurement of the light we perceive. (See also description on page 25.)

CDM (ceramic discharge metal-halide)
A light source that contains an electric discharge within a ceramic cylinder. The ceramic improves the stability of the discharge by providing a light source with a more reliable and repeatable colour temperature and colour stability than traditional metal-halide sources.

colour temperature
Phenomenon by which incandescent materials release energy as electromagnetic radiation when heated. When the material reaches a high enough temperature, it becomes 'red hot' and begins to produce electromagnetic radiation as visible light. As temperature increases, the light from the incandescent source produces more and more short wavelength radiation, and so becomes bluer. White light sources are classified by the temperature that a perfect black-body (**incandescent**) radiator has to be heated to in order to produce white light of an equivalent hue. Colour temperature is measured on the **Kelvin** scale.

DALI (Digital Addressable Lighting Interface)
An open standard describing a protocol and electrical system for control of networked luminaires. A DALI network will consist of a controller and one or more controlled devices. DALI devices are commonly dimmers or dimmable ballast controllers for fluorescent lamps. DALI devices can provide grouped or individual control of devices. DALI is not a fast protocol and is therefore often used for lighting systems that do not require rapid changes, or where minor timing variations are non-critical, such as in office environments.

diffuser
A diffusing material that disperses or scatters light. Incident light can be diffused by reflective or transmissive materials. A theoretically ideal diffusely reflecting surface (known as a Lambertian surface) will produce a reflection pattern with equal intensity in all directions. A sheet of white paper is a good example of a nearly Lambertian reflector. Transmissive diffusing materials allow a beam of light to pass through while softening the beam. Mist, fog, clouds, tracing paper, etched glass, frosted glass and opaline glass are all examples of transmissive materials that diffuse light to a lesser or greater extent.

discharge light source
Visible light produced by an electric discharge through a gas. This process can be used to produce visible light directly or indirectly, by producing **ultraviolet** radiation that is converted into visible light by fluorescent materials (see description on page 50).

DMX (Digital Multiplex)
A digital protocol used primarily for communicating with lighting equipment. Most commonly used in theatre and stage lighting, it operates very rapidly, allowing fast changes in lighting levels or the positions of motors controlling focus or the positions of luminaires. DMX allows 512 separate channels of data to be transmitted, with 256 steps per channel (8 bits per channel). Larger DMX control installations use multiple 'universes' of 512 channels.

DSI (Digital Signal Interface)
A lighting control protocol. It is a proprietary system and has largely been superseded by the **DALI** open standard.

electroluminescent (EL)
A type of light source consisting of flat sheets of flexible material that produce light when an electrical current is passed across them. They are typically found as backlights to mobile phone screens, wristwatches and vehicle instrument panels. This technology is not capable of producing light sources with a high luminous intensity and it has limited application in architectural lighting. **LED**s are another form of electroluminescent light source (see page 55).

electromagnetic (EM) radiation
A form of energy that travels in synchronized waves of electric and magnetic fields. Electromagnetic radiation is classified by the frequency of the wave that carries the energy – higher frequency waves carry more energy. Light is a form of electromagnetic energy that we perceive visually. The electromagnetic spectrum contains all forms of EM radiant energy and includes radio waves, microwaves, **infrared**, visible light, **ultraviolet**, X-rays and gamma rays.

filter
Typically a transparent material used to alter the colour or beam shape of light passing through it. Theatrical filters are commonly produced as thin flexible sheets of dyed polycarbonate or polyester film that are easily cut to size to sit in front of a luminaire to colour or soften the light. These materials are temporary solutions that fade and degrade over time. Permanent filters use glass substrates.

high pressure discharge light source
See **discharge light source**, and page 54.

illuminance
Term to describe the light that falls on a surface. We do not see illuminance – what we see is **luminance** (the light reflected by the surface). The light reflected will be a proportion of the illuminance. A white surface that receives the same illuminance as a black surface will reflect more light and have a greater luminance (or, in visual terms, it will appear brighter). The SI unit for illuminance is **lux**.

incandescent
A type of light source in which an element is heated until it glows (see page 49).

infrared
The portion of the electromagnetic spectrum with wavelengths just higher than the maximum sensitivity of the human visual system. We cannot see infrared radiation, but we do experience it as heat.

isolux diagram
Diagram used to display the light distribution of a **luminaire** (see page 65).

Kelvin
SI base unit of temperature. On the Kelvin scale, zero represents the point at which all thermal motion ceases. This is referred to as absolute zero as there is no lower temperature. In lighting, the Kelvin scale is used to define the apparent **colour temperature** (see page 53).

lamp
The common name for a light source.

LED (light emitting diode)
A semiconductor light source that produces light by an electroluminescent process. Because LEDs are small, the light produced can be focused more easily than with larger light sources. LEDs produce very little heat compared with **incandescent** light sources, but they are very sensitive to excess heat and light output and their longevity can be diminished severely if they are allowed to overheat.

lens
A concave or convex piece of transparent material (usually glass) used to converge or diverge a beam of light through the process of **refraction**. In lighting, lenses are often used to focus a beam of light or to create a projected image.

light meter (or **illuminance meter**)
A device used to measure the quantity of visible light that falls on a surface. An illuminance meter will usually give results in **lux** or footcandles. Illuminance meters are usually designed to respond to visible light in a similar way to the photopic response of the human visual system. As such, they do not give an absolute measure of **luminous flux**, but a figure weighted by the relative sensitivity of our visual system.

lumen
The SI base unit of **luminous flux**. It is a description of the quantity of light either produced by a source or incident on a surface. One lumen is the quantity of luminous flux emitted within a solid angle of one **steradian** emitted by a uniform light source that has a luminous intensity of one **candela**.

luminaire
A complete light fitting, including the light source, reflector, any lenses and its housing.

luminance
The intensity of light produced by a **luminaire** or reflected from a surface.

luminous flux
The rate of flow of visible light energy. The SI base unit for luminous flux is the **lumen**.

lux
The SI base unit of **illuminance**. It is equal to one **lumen** per square metre.

nanometre
A unit of length equivalent to one billionth of a metre.

OLED (organic light emitting diode)
A flat panel device that produces visible light by a process of electroluminescence.

prism
A transparent solid in the form of an extruded triangle. Typically made of glass or other optically clear material, the non-parallel geometry of the sides is responsible for the **refraction** of light. Triangular prisms can refract light to display the spectrum of colours contained within white light.

Rayleigh scattering
The scattering of visible light by particles suspended in a transparent medium. Typically this involves small particles in the atmosphere interacting with sunlight. In the upper atmosphere, the blue end of the spectrum is scattered most strongly and so produces the appearance of a blue sky.

receptor A light-sensitive cell that responds to **electromagnetic radiation** in the visible light spectrum.

refraction
The process by which electromagnetic waves are deflected when passing obliquely between transparent media of differing densities. This is demonstrated when light passes though the curved glass of an optical **lens**.

saccadic movement
An involuntary process of rapid eye movements that allows the eye to scan its region of highest resolution (the fovea) over several parts of a scene.

sculpture lens (aka spread lens)
An optical device that does not spread light symmetrically. When used on a symmetrical spotlight, a sculpture lens can stretch a beam of light vertically without spreading it horizontally – making it ideal for illuminating vertical objects such as tall sculptures. The lens can be used in any orientation to spread the light in any direction required.

specular reflector
A reflective material that has the properties of a mirror. Specular reflectors reflect light at an equal and opposite angle to the incident beam of light. The reflected light from a specular reflector will exhibit a distinct direction to the reflected beam of light. Compare with a **diffuser**.

steradian
The SI unit of a solid angle.

stereo vision
The process by which the visual system combines separate views from two eyes to create depth perception.

translucent
Term used to describe a material, for example frosted glass, that allows diffuse light to pass through it.

transparent
Term used to describe a material, for example clear glass, that allows light to pass through it. An opaque material, for example a piece of card, is the opposite of transparent and will allow no light to pass through.

ultraviolet (UV)
Part of the visible spectrum, the wavelength of ultraviolet is shorter than violet but longer than that of X-rays. Although invisible to the human eye, UV light (also known as black light) emits long wave radiation and causes white (and some coloured) materials to fluoresce. UV is a component of sunlight, but the ozone layer prevents much of it from reaching the earth's surface.

veiling reflection
Where users are working with objects with reflective surfaces, such as computer screens or even glossy magazines, bright surfaces or luminaires can be reflected into the eyes of the viewer. These reflections not only obscure parts of the objects being viewed, but can also reduce the general contrast between the light and dark areas of the object – literally drawing a luminous veil over it.

Further reading

Armstrong, T. and Bear, M., *Colour Perception: A Practical Approach to Colour Theory*, Tarquin Publications, St Albans, 1991

Boyce, P. and Raynham, P., *The SLL Lighting Handbook*, Chartered Institution of Building Services Engineers, London, 2009

Clegg, B., *Light Years: The Extraordinary Story of Mankind's Fascination with Light*, Piatkus Books, London, 2001

Cumming, R. and Porter, T., *The Colour Eye*, BBC Books, London, 1991

Cuttle, C., *Lighting by Design*, Architectural Press, Oxford, 2004

Downer, J., *Supersense: Perception in the Animal World*, BBC Books, London, 1988

Gregory, R. L., *Eye and Brain: The Psychology of Seeing*, fifth edition, Oxford University Press, Oxford, 1997

Keller, M., *Light Fantastic: The Art and Design of Stage Lighting*, second edition, Prestel, London, 2000

Lam, W. M., *Perception and Lighting as Formgivers for Architecture*. McGraw-Hill Inc., New York, 1977

Major, M., Speirs, J. and Tischhauser, A., *Made of Light: The Art of Light and Architecture*, Birkhäuser, Basel, 2005

Minnaert, M., *Light and Color in the Outdoors*, Springer, New York/Berlin/Heidelberg, 1995

Mueller, C. G. and Rudolph, M., *Light and Vision*, Time, Inc., New York, 1966

Porter, T. and Mikellides, B., *Colour for Architecture Today*, Taylor & Francis, London, 2008

Storey, S., *Lighting by Design*, Pavilion Books, London, 2002

Zajonc, A., *Catching the Light: The Entwined History of Light and Mind*, Oxford University Press, New York and Oxford, 1995

Index

Picture credits

Front cover Image based on an original drawing by molo, showing their cloud + urchin softlights and softwall luminous partition wall

Back cover Malcolm Innes

1 Paul Zanne/Gavin Fraser, FOTO-MA

3 Anne Bureau Concepteur Lumière

6 Malcolm Innes

7 top flickr.com/photos/hibino

7 bottom Malcolm Innes

8 Malcolm Innes

10 Metaveld bv

11–23 Malcolm Innes

26 flickr.com/photos/karen_roe

27–33 Malcolm Innes

36 flickr.com/photos/franciscoferreira

37 left Malcolm Innes

37 right flickr.com/photos/davidden

38–44 Malcolm Innes

45 top right Malcolm Innes

45 centre left flickr.com/3059349393

45 centre right flickr.com/elenaacin

45 bottom left flickr.com/photos/leonizzy

45 bottom right flickr.com/whiskeyandtears

46 Speirs and Major Associates

47 top Speirs and Major Associates

47 bottom left and right Malcolm Innes

48 flickr.com/SF Brit

49 Malcolm Innes

51 Wikimedia Commons/Jurii

52–53 Malcolm Innes

54 Malcolm Innes

55 Xicato

56 Malcolm Innes

58–59 Malcolm Innes

60–69 Malcolm Innes

71 Timothy Soar

72 Malcolm Innes

74–79 Malcolm Innes

80 left Malcolm Innes

80 right Kevan Shaw Lighting Design

81 top Malcolm Innes

81 bottom Kevan Shaw Lighting Design

82 Kevan Shaw Lighting Design

83–86 Malcolm Innes

87 Focus Lighting

89 flickr.com/photos/seier

90 left Giovanni Vincenti/iStockphoto

90 right Malcolm Innes

91 Malcolm Innes

92 top flickr.com/photos/afferent

92 bottom left and right Malcolm Innes

93–95 Malcolm Innes

96 top ©David Kilpatrick/Alamy

96 bottom ©Olli Geibel/Alamy

97 top ©Peter D. O'Neill TW:EEC/Alamy

97 bottom flickr.com/photos/etherealdawn

98 Malcolm Innes

100 Kevan Shaw Lighting Design

101 Malcolm Innes

102 flickr.com/photos/afferent

103 Alex Poldavo (flickr.com/photos/poldavo)

104 top Richard Winchell (flickr.com/photos/richardwinchell)

104 bottom Speirs and Major Associates

105 Speirs and Major Associates

106 Kevan Shaw Lighting Design

107 Malcolm Innes

108–109 Malcolm Innes

110–112 Paul Zanne/Gavin Fraser, FOTO-MA

113 right Malcolm Innes

114–115 Alan Toft (courtesy Speirs and Major Associates)

116–117 Speirs and Major Associates

118–119 Alan Toft (courtesy Speirs and Major Associates)

120 Malcolm Innes

121 Hélène Binet

122 Focus Lighting/J.R. Krauza

123 David M. Joseph

124–125 Focus Lighting

128 Malcolm Innes

130–138 Malcolm Innes

140 Sarah Kidd, Edinburgh Napier University

141 Emily Davies, Edinburgh Napier University

142–144 Malcolm Innes

145 Kevan Shaw Lighting Design

146–147 Malcolm Innes

148 Speirs and Major Associates

149–151 Malcolm Innes

152–153 Speirs and Major Associates/Rogers Stirk Harbour + Partners, Estudio Lamella

154–155 Kevan Shaw Lighting Design

156 Malcolm Innes

157 Focus Lighting

158 Malcolm Innes

159 Anne Bureau Concepteur Lumière

160 top Malcolm Innes

160 bottom Anne Bureau Concepteur Lumière

161 top Malcolm Innes

161 bottom Anne Bureau Concepteur Lumière

162 Sharon O'Connor

163 Anne Bureau Concepteur Lumière

164–165 OVI (Office for Visual Interaction)

166 Kevan Shaw Lighting Design

167 Malcolm Innes

168 top Sharon O'Connor

168 bottom Kevan Shaw Lighting Design

169 Sharon O'Connor

170 OVI (Office for Visual Interaction)

171 redrawn based on original image courtesy OVI

174–175 Malcolm Innes

178–179 *Multiverse* (2008) by Leo Villareal. Photo: ©David Coleman/Alamy

180–181 Malcolm Innes

182 Malcolm Innes

Acknowledgements

I would like to thank all the contributors who made this book possible. In particular, thanks go to Paul Gregory, Anne Bureau, Jean Sundin, Gavin Fraser, Kevan Shaw, Mark Major, Jonathan Speirs and Keith Bradshaw for permission to use their projects as case studies. Thanks also to Iain Ruxton for his numerous forays into the archives to find drawings, images and facts.

I would like to thank Heather Christie for her patient encouragement and boundless emotional support. She also proved to be an invaluable sounding board for ideas and an insightful reader, identifying errors, omissions and plain nonsense. Without her support, the project could not have happened – I am always in her debt.

I would also like to recognize that the lighting knowledge and design approaches described in this book were developed over many years working with Kevan Shaw and then Jonathan Speirs and Mark Major; some of the greatest lighting design practitioners I could have hoped to work with. I was constantly inspired by the projects we worked on, but even more inspiring was the group of deeply talented and creative colleagues I worked alongside.

Architectural lighting designers often exhibit a huge breadth of knowledge and experience beyond architectural lighting. The resulting 'alternative view' that this leads to is one of the great strengths of the profession. I continue to be stimulated by the projects and publications of lighting's many technical wizards, the lighting poets and the artists of light who create carefully crafted compositions of light and shade. Lighting inspiration comes from many directions – take them all.

Finally, I would like to acknowledge the contribution of clients, architects, interior designers, other design professionals and manufacturers who collectively contribute so much to the success of a great project. Our failures often teach us more than our successes – thank you to all those who have provided those learning opportunities.